PRELIMINARY ESSAYS

PRELIMINARY ESSAYS

by
JOHN WAIN

LONDON
MACMILLAN & CO LTD
NEW YORK · ST MARTIN'S PRESS
1957

PR 99
.W25

MACMILLAN AND COMPANY LIMITED
London Bombay Calcutta Madras Melbourne

THE MACMILLAN COMPANY OF CANADA LIMITED
Toronto

ST MARTIN'S PRESS INC
New York

*Printed in Great Britain by Richard Clay and Company, Ltd.,
Bungay, Suffolk*

AL'S

These essays, in part or whole, appeared in the following periodicals, whose editors and publishers are thanked for permission to reprint: *Essays in Criticism, The London Magazine, Mandrake, Penguin New Writing, The Spectator* and *The Twentieth Century.*

CONTENTS

. . . what marked and striking excellence has England to shew to make her civilisation attractive? Her literature is one of her excellences and attractions and I believe that criticism will tend to make this more and more felt; but there must be more of that literature, a continued supply and in quality excellent.

— Hopkins to Coventry Patmore,
June 4, 1886.

PREFACE

Any collection of critical essays is rather like a diary. Over the years, the critic tries to clarify and express his view of the various books, authors, and topics that have, for one reason or another, compelled his attention. Finally the day comes when he gathers up a sheaf of these attempts and looks through them; if he has developed at all, he is bound to catch himself thinking, now and again, as he does so: 'Did I really say this?' But the mere fact of having developed has also taught him that it would be useless to begin tinkering, trying to bring every essay up to date in terms of his current ideas and preferences. It would take months, and at the end he would only be in the position of the men who are permanently employed in painting the Forth Bridge; the beginning would have to be done again, 'and so *ad infinitum*'. So he either gives up the idea of bringing out a collection, or leaves it as a diary, appending dates to the essays like the photographs in the family album.

Even working on this plan, I have to admit that one or two of these essays are frankly included as period pieces. The essay on Mr. Empson's poetry, for instance, is here because, clumsy as it is, it *did* something: it helped to trigger off the vogue for his work that has been such a feature of the literary history of the 1950's; it therefore has some interest as a document. In the same way, I thought it better to reprint my review of Dylan Thomas's *Collected Poems* than to start all over again with a new essay; my view of his work has not greatly altered, and I have a strong feeling (perhaps partly due to my academic training) that a comment made on the spot, while the thing was brand-new, has documentary value; it has the power to reveal something about the period it dates from, which the wisest retrospective comment may lack.

Most of the essays, however, are in the book either because I still agree with what I said in them and could not put it better now, or because, though no longer in agreement, I am in hopes of getting some reaction to the point I was making. Criticism thrives on the clash of opinions, and, in the words of Kafka's epigram, 'From a real adversary boundless courage flows into one.'

Finally, the book is called 'Preliminary' because it takes a long time to learn to become a critic, and I have only been at it for ten years. We throw the word 'critic' about, nowadays, rather recklessly; any *flâneur*, however ignorant and presumptuous, who has done his bit of book-reviewing is 'Mr. X, the critic'; but, in my view, it is a title to be earned. These essays are the record of part of an apprenticeship; I cannot tell when, if ever, that apprenticeship will be over.

J. W.

RESTORATION COMEDY AND ITS
MODERN CRITICS

I

THE comment one finds oneself making on most Restoration plays is not so much literary-critical as sociological. I know, of course, that this is true of most minor literature; the only sane reason for ploughing through the mass of hacked-out Elizabethan plays or third-rate Victorian novels, or forcing a path through pages of stiff Augustan couplets, is to increase the sensitiveness of our 'feel' for those periods; obviously, the more we read, whether of good or bad, the more naturally we inhabit the age we are studying. Obviously, too, there is this element of the sociological, or social-historical, in all reading; the greatest author is a fact that happened in history, like the greatest Prime Minister or general; it is merely a question of having the tact to use this information in the right way, and this tact is something we have to be born with. I heap up these very elementary remarks because they are the first essentials of an approach to Restoration stage comedy. Viewed in the mass, it calls for no comment beyond an acknowledgement of its diagnostic value; without it, we should find it that much harder to understand the mind of the English governing class after 1660; but even so it would not be impossible; we should still have Pepys's diary and the memoirs of Grammont and Dryden's poems. What Restoration comedy does reveal, more than any other source, is the extent to which people were unbalanced; like Dada, for instance, it was the fever-chart of a sick society, a society that might easily have died.

Most of the historical side of the discussion, too — the arguments about whether Restoration comedy derives from the French, or whether it is a continuation of tendencies that were visible before the theatres closed, or what precise blend of the two — most of this seems to me likewise to be largely socio-logical. Whatever the experts decide won't alter the position much; of course there had been a fashion in Charles I's time for going to private theatres and paying more to get in, so that the theatre had ceased to be broadly popular as it was in Shakespeare's day (what a lot of advantages Shakespeare had, after all!); and of course the exiled courtiers had spent a fair stretch of time in France, and would naturally want to introduce into their own literature some of the things they had learnt there. On the formal side, it is clear that Restoration comedy could hardly have developed in any other way than as it did: 'witty', immoral, and reflecting class interests.[1]

I say 'immoral' because this comedy is one of the symptoms of a sick society, and one of the things that society was sick of, naturally, was too much morality. That point we can take as read. It is the overall picture that is interesting. The seventeenth century was the time when the English made the basic discoveries about what kind of modern nation they were going to turn into. Within that hundred years, attempt after attempt was made to blueprint a completely new society. The Civil War was a gigantic clash between the inherited, romantic attitudes of feudalism, and the practical hard head of business-like respectability. The inherited feudalism went down, and that ought to have been the end of the Middle Ages — but it wasn't. The respectable hard heads, left in power, tried to run England as a modern state, by means of a centralized military despotism backed by enforced respectability, like an Eastern European country today. They failed, because the

[1] Shirley's *The Witty Fair One* (1628) offers this passage, which can stand in token of all the scores that exist, to illustrate the incidence of 'Restoration' atti-tudes and mannerisms before the Civil War: 'There is no discourse so becoming your gallants now, as a horse race, or Hyde-park, — what ladies' lips are softest, what fashion is most terse and courtly, what news abroad, which is the best vaulting-house, where shall we taste canary and be drunk tonight? talk of morality! — here be ladies still, you shall hear me court one of them; I hope you will not report abroad among my friends that I love her; it is the love of mount-ing into her maidenhead, I vow, Jack, and nothing else.' Significantly, this play was revived in 1666.

English cannot, ultimately, be ruled by business minds; they are too romantic, too hungry for tradition, too snobbish, and too hostile to anything logical and time-saving. If the Commonwealth had been a success, England today would be something like, say, Switzerland. The difference shows the extent to which it failed. The next expedient was to put the inherited feudal society back on its feet, but with a number of safeguards on either side. It was an incredibly difficult situation, especially as neither party could really assess the amount of give and take that would be necessary. Charles II was, in this respect, an almost complete flop; at the end of his reign English society was faced with all the same problems it had been faced with at the beginning.

But we must let that pass. The situation cannot be blamed on the King. When a society is in an *impasse*, the responsibility for helping it out of that *impasse* rests on every person who lives in it, in greater proportion as he is more influential. Artists are especially influential and their responsibility is enormous. The main social problem, in day-to-day living, was the clash of attitudes between the restored aristocratic mentality and the ever-strengthening business mentality. The courtier, having been driven out by force of arms and then re-admitted by force of bargaining, was naturally on the defensive; his pride had been hurt. The citizen, confident of his ability to manage practical affairs (*i.e.* keep his shop so that his shop would keep him), was less confident of having all the answers as regards the kind of society that they were both trying to engineer. He looked at the courtier with a blend of resentment, fear, and envy. Two utterly contrasting types were trying to rub along together.

The immediate result on English literature was that it became bifurcated as never before or since. When we speak of 'Restoration' literature, we usually mean upper-class, metropolitan Restoration literature; properly speaking, we should equally well be referring to — for example — Bunyan, all of whose works, with the exception of *Some Gospel Truths* (1656), were published after the Restoration; or, for that matter, to Milton. The thing fell into two halves, which is a sure sign of an unhealthy national life. But without the evidence of the drama, we should hardly realize the extent of this split. After all, in most other branches of literature — scientific prose, history, poetry — men of diverse attitudes had *some* common ground they could meet on. It was the theatre that carried partisan spirit furthest. Here we reach the nature of the sociological interest that Restoration comedy has for us; it is not even *trying* to be impartial, or to make any constructive suggestion. At its usual level, it is partly a yell of triumph — 'We're back, and the King's back, and we'll see you don't forget it' — and partly a prolonged indulgence in wish-fulfilling fantasy. The man of fashion and leisure, even with the approval of the Court behind him, was not quite so sure of himself as he wanted to seem. Even though there had been a Restoration, things were not quite the same. It was natural that he should enjoy seeing plays in which men like himself were automatically wittier, handsomer and more successful than his anti-type, the 'cit'. He liked watching himself being a devil with the women, too clever for the merchant, superior to the Puritan, and occasionally dressing up as a clergyman as a means to seducing someone's wife — just to show what he thought of clergymen. And the sort of woman he took with him enjoyed it too; it confirmed her in her way of life. The success of this rather pitiful bravado is one pointer to the reason why most Restoration comedy is so bad; it was aimed at a prepared audience, who knew in advance what they wanted.

To confirm this, we need only read through the Prologues and Epilogues in which the dramatists addressed their audience without intermediary. Usually, these are labelled, 'Spoken by Mr. (or Mrs.) So-and-so', as if to underline that the personality of the player was an important element in the mixture; the actress demurely speaking libidinous verses was, of course, part of what the audience paid for. But what I am primarily thinking of is this kind of thing:

Ah! Happy you, with Ease and with Delight,
Who act those Follies, Poets toil to write!
The sweating Muse does almost leave the chace,
She puffs, and hardly keeps your *Protean* Vices pace.
Pinch you but in one Vice, away you fly
To some new Frisk of contrariety.

You rowle like Snow-Balls, gathering as you run,
And get seven Dev'ls, when dispossess'd of one.
Your *Venus* once was a *Platonique* Queen,
Nothing of Love beside the Face was seen;
But every Inch of Her you now Uncase,
And clap a Vizard-Masque upon the Face.

This is from the Epilogue to Thomas Southerne's *The Disappointment* (1684). I cannot claim great erudition, by the way, for digging up this kind of thing; it is all in one book, Professor Nell Wiley's *Rare Prologues and Epilogues, 1642–1700* (1940).

Isolated as it was, the Restoration theatre was still further split. There was a crack running right down the centre of it, between tragedy and comedy: impossibly high-flown emotionalism about Love and Honour on the one hand, the repudiation of all standards on the other. Restoration comedy is thus a segment of a segment. We cannot study it, as we can Elizabethan drama or the Victorian novel, in the hope of finding clues to the attitude of a society as a whole. It is a piece broken off one half of a split mind.

In this sense, Restoration comedy is part of the literature of the Civil War; it has all the animosity of the battlefield in its heart. It is, of course, precisely this quality that makes it an essential starting-point for the study of the Augustan age. Why is early eighteenth-century English literature so largely, almost entirely, pre-occupied with conduct? Here is part of the answer; this un-healed split between two worlds, which had, nevertheless, to cohere somehow if — as was now established — neither of them could eliminate the other. Fifty and sixty years later, the split was still visible, but it was healing, and it is to the credit of the men of letters that they devoted so much energy to helping forward the healing process. Pope's Moral Essays, Chesterfield's Letters, the torrent of periodical writing, all sought to give more or less sensible advice about how to live within the bounds of a decent compromise. Chesterfield sometimes makes himself sound a little like Congreve's Lord Froth ('But there is nothing more unbecoming a Man of Quality, than to Laugh; 'tis such a vulgar Expression of the Passions! every Body can laugh. Then especially to laugh at the Jest of an inferior Person, or when any body else of the same Quality does not laugh with one; ridiculous!'), but he did sketch an acceptable code of aristocratic *mores*; Addison may seem too mealy-mouthed in his attitude towards the British Merchant of his day, but he did set Sir Andrew Freeport and Will Honeycomb round the same dinner-table, and this was good medicine.

This was all something of an uphill struggle. What chiefly strikes one on dipping into the *Tatler* and *Spectator* is the extent to which Restoration attitudes survived into the eighteenth century; admittedly, it was no longer fashionable (if it ever had been) to behave like Rochester, but such anecdotes as the following (*Spectator*, 154) were probably not much exaggerated:

> You are to know then that I was bred a Gentleman, and had the finishing Part of my Education under a Man of great Probity, Wit, and Learning in one of our Universities. I will not deny but this made my Behaviour and Mien bear in it a Figure of Thought rather than Action; and a Man of a quite contrary Character, who never thought in his Life, rallied me one Day upon it, and said, He believ'd I was still a Virgin. There was a young Lady of Virtue present, and I was not displeased to favour the Insinuation: but it had a quite contrary Effect from what I expected; I was ever after treated with great Coldness both by that Lady and all the rest of my Acquaintance. In a very little Time I never came into a Room but I could hear a Whisper, Here comes the Maid: A Girl of Humour would on some Occasion say, Why how do you know more than any of us? An Expression of that kind was generally followed by a loud Laugh! In a Word, for no other Fault in the World than that they really thought

me as innocent as themselves, I became of no Consequence among them, and was receiv'd always upon the Foot of a Jest. This made so strong an Impression upon me, that I resolv'd to be as agreeable as the best of the Men who laugh'd at me; but I observed it was Nonsense for me to be impudent at first among those who knew me: My Character for Modesty was so notorious wherever I had hitherto appeared, that I resolved to shew my new Face in new Quarters of the World. My first Step I chose with Judgment, for I went to *Astrop*; and came down among a Crowd of Academicks, at one Dash, the impudentest Fellow they had ever seen in their Lives. Flushed with this Success, I made Love and was happy. Upon this Conquest I thought it would be unlike a Gentleman to stay long with my Mistress, and crossed the Country to *Bury*: I could give you a very good Account of myself at that Place also.

II

But is this really all one has to say about Restoration comedy? That it provides documentation of the split that was later to be healed by the efforts of men like Addison? As I started by saying, this is all there is to the common run of it, the mass of more or less rubbishy stage-fodder produced by people like Aphra Behn and Ravenscroft; but there are one or two points at which Restoration comedy abuts on to literature; one or two plays, or passages in plays, where one suddenly finds oneself in the presence of a genuine moral issue or a flicker of living emotion.

This, by rights, ought to be where we turn to the critics. If ever the literary critic — the man who has trained himself in the right kind of discrimination — could be useful to us, here, one would have said, was his chance. And yet, on turning to the shelves, one finds an odd lack: not, indeed, of quantity — there never is a lack of quantity — but of quality. Our best critics have mostly left the subject alone, as much as to say that it simply did not seem interesting enough to them. On the other hand, there are the books devoted to this or that Restoration author, which nearly all over-praise their subjects. In fact, one has to read some

B

of these special studies to know what overpraise really is. In D. Crane Taylor's *William Congreve*, for instance, a book which has all the solemn weight of an Oxford imprint, there are passages where, even if we substituted the name 'Shakespeare' for the name 'Congreve', we should still think he was drawing the long bow a little. One thinks, again, of the determination with which the late Montague Summers tossed the superlatives about when discussing the blowsiest Restoration play; he is so committed to praising everything he finds in *The Country Wife*, for instance, that when faced with the character of Harcourt, which the author has simply left as a cardboard cut-out, his comment is that 'Wycherley with consummate art has left Ned Harcourt a sketch for the actor to fill in' (*The Playhouse of Pepys*, chap. IV). This kind of 'consummate art' isn't rare in the poorest Hollywood films. Then there is Professor Dobrée's curious overpraise of Congreve, in his so useful and so often-quoted *Restoration Comedy*, in terms of cadences, rhythmical balance, and what-not. Congreve had a good ear for idiosyncrasies of speech, and knew how to write sentences that are short and rhythmical and sound well when spoken from the stage, but so did the author of *Charley's Aunt*. 'For sinewy flexibility and point, combined with seductive gentleness; for the full gamut of vowel sounds and the varied spacing of stresses, English literature had to wait for Landor until it once more heard a voice that had something of the especial quality of Congreve,' Professor Dobrée writes. With all due respect, I doubt whether this is more than an emphatic way of saying that Congreve knew how to write good prose. It is very puzzling; one cannot get away from the feeling that Congreve is being boosted rather than assessed; yet why should this be? Take another example from Professor Dobrée (this and the last quotation both come from the Introduction to his edition of Congreve in the World's Classics):

> To give only one example of how, by phrasing alone, he could alter the speed, it will be enough to point out the staggering finale of

The Double Dealer. The play has been proceeding at a glorious and
ever-increasing pace; until the last moment we are borne along in a
tremendous rush; it seems incredible that the curtain should not
come down upon a tumult: but then:

> *Brisk.* This is all very surprising, let me perish!
> *Lady Froth.* You know I told you Saturn looked a little more
> angry than usual.

This shows his strength: we are suddenly pulled up sharp.

One turns up the passage and looks at it again. Staggering,
certainly, but not in the sense that it staggers us; in the sense that
it is off balance and about to fall. The whole play is full of
disastrous and jarring changes of mood, owing to the presence of
irreconcilable elements; in the last scene, everything is being tidied
up in perfunctory haste; it seems incredible that the curtain should
not come down because one can feel Congreve's boredom and
exasperation with the silly mess he has got his play into; and then
the two comic characters each throw in a line. Isn't it just a stock
device of stage farce? Doesn't the comic man always say 'Gor-
blimey' when the missing jewels are discovered at the bottom of
the baronet's inkwell? And does this *really* show 'strength' of anything like an individual kind?

But still there remains one's rather baffling sense, after reading
through a number of these comedies, that they have, after all,
some merit; that, even if one cannot join in the attempt to deck
them out as great literature on aesthetic grounds, there is some
case to be made out for them. An obvious exception to my remark
that the best critics have tended to ignore the subject is, of course,
the celebrated essay by L. C. Knights, the only attention (so far as
I know) that any of the *Scrutiny* group has paid to it.[1] Professor
Knights is, to my mind, much the best writer on Restoration
comedy, the only one who sets about the subject in the manner
of a man accustomed to dealing with literature in a valid way; and
his essay consists of a blistering attack on it! Some parts of this

---

[1] *Explorations* (1947), pp. 131–49.

attack I find not altogether convincing; the claim that the prose of these dramatists is poor and malnourished by comparison with the non-dramatic prose of the period is one that can be made out easily enough by juggling with quotations, and answered by juggling with more quotations; I don't think the general impression would bear out this marked separation of the two. But the main points are made with a vigour that, since it has gone un-· answered, we must call unanswerable. Professor Knights finds Restoration comedy impoverished, in view of the wider sweep of life that it might have taken in. He admits, of course, that if much of the Elizabethan richness had been lost, something had also been gained, in point, precision, and intellectual curiosity; but, to him, these comedies merely gesture in the direction of this curiosity, and remain content to deal in a few stock notions. 'The trouble,' he says, 'is not that the Restoration comic writers deal with a limited number of themes, but that they bring to bear a miserably limited set of attitudes.'

If I do not quite feel that this is the last word, this is not because I have found some formula to dissolve Professor Knights's criticism. Nor has anyone else. Mr. Clifford Leech[1] suggests rather timidly, in a footnote, that here and there 'the implied attitudes seem more complex than this, more detached from the general playhouse intentions'; but I think it is a moot point whether he has really established this, helpful as his essay is. More recently Mr. Marvin Mudrick, in an essay on 'Restoration Comedy and Later',[2] puts up his gloves to Professor Knights with more show of aggression, but since he pins his thesis to the argument that, after all, Restoration comedy isn't so much worse than Elizabethan comedy, because Shakespeare's comedies are not much good, so that only leaves Jonson, he doesn't help much. After a few circles round the plays, we reach the important truth that 'the comedy of manners does not necessarily trifle; it is hospitable to

[1] *Essays in Criticism*, Vol. I, No. 2, pp. 165–84.
[2] In *English Stage Comedy*. English Institute Essays, 1954, ed. W. K. Wimsatt. Columbia, 1955.

serious issues'. I don't think Professor Knights need feel that he should climb down in deference to *these* arguments.

Paradoxically enough, the boldest blast on a pro-Restoration bugle has been sounded from Hawaii, where Professor Thomas H. Fujimura, in his book *The Restoration Comedy of Wit* (1952), has no intention of giving an inch, and lays about him mightily in defence of Etherege, Wycherley, and Congreve. It is the more to be regretted that he does not seem to have heard of Professor Knights; the very full bibliography at the end of the book does not include Knights's essay, though it has room for everything else, down to Ellehauge's more or less worthless *English Restoration Drama* of 1933. Since Professor Fujimura is about the most whole-hearted defender that these playwrights have found since their own day, the spectacle is an oddly disappointing one, like the career of a heavyweight whose manager arranges for him to fight everyone except the reigning champion. His book is, I think, the best introduction to the subject, if only for the care with which he fills in the background; his chapter on 'The Nature of Wit' argues convincingly that the life and soul of Restoration comedy was 'wit', a word to which the period attached two chief meanings: first, decorum, and getting things into their right proportions; second, aptness in finding images and metaphors (on this side it is linked with the wit of the Metaphysicals; he might have mentioned that this double sense was still alive in Johnson's day, as is shown by the fact that Johnson's two chief definitions of wit are 'that which, upon its first production, is immediately acknowledged to be just', and 'the unexpected copulation of ideas' — two entirely separate definitions, yet both surviving even in the impoverished modern notion of wit as intellectual agility manifested in the ability to make a special kind of joke). Professor Fujimura suggests that Restoration comedy should be known by the general title of 'Comedy of Wit', rather than of 'Manners', and this seems reasonable. The rest of his argument, however, seems to be pitched too high. In his second chapter, 'The Intellectual

Background of Wit Comedy', he argues that these plays express an attitude to life that can be paralleled in much of the thinking that was going on around them; Hobbes gave people the notion of man as a pleasure-seeking machine, so that Burnet thought it a disaster that the King should be so thick with him and pick up his wicked ideas. Certainly the sort of thing Mr. Fujimura quotes from Hobbes is pretty powerful and would quickly influence anyone whose bent was towards libertinism in the first place, *e.g.*:

> Every man, for his own part, calleth that which *pleaseth*, and is delightful to himself, *good*; and that *evil* which *displeaseth* him: insomuch that while every man *differeth* from another in *constitution*, they differ also from one another concerning the common distinction of good and evil. Nor is there any such thing as absolute goodness, considered without relation (*Human Nature*, VII, 3).

Anyone with the slightest acquaintance with the period will allow Mr. Fujimura his point that 'the naturalism, libertinism, and scepticism of wit comedy spring from the naturalistic and sceptical temper of the age'. But it still seems a bit of a jump from there to his next point: 'It is clear that the writers of wit comedy were not immoral and profane, as the casual reader unfamiliar with the intellectual temper of the age would assume'. The idea seems to be that as long as everyone else was just as bad, or likely at any moment to be just as bad, this put the comic writers in the clear; but I think such reasoning on Mr. Fujimura's part must be the result of all those quotations from Hobbes he has been copying out. Indeed he goes to amusing lengths to establish that the never-ending stream of filth that splashes across the stage, in these plays, is all right because it is 'wit'. Even the *mores* of the time are redeemed because people were witty, and this doctrine is doubly comforting since the standard of wit he applies is not at all a high one. As an instructive contrast, compare Macaulay and Professor Fujimura on a well-known episode in the life of Wycherley; his escapade with the Duchess of Cleveland. Here is Macaulay:

The Duchess admired him, and proceeded to make love to him, after the fashion of the coarse-minded and shameless circle to which she belonged. In the Ring, when the crowd of beauties and fine gentlemen was thickest, she put her head out of her coach-window, and bawled to him, 'Sir, you are a rascal; you are a villain;' and, if she is not belied, she added another phrase of abuse which we will not quote, but of which we may say that it might most justly have been applied to her own children. Wycherley called on her Grace the next day, and with great humility begged to know in what way he had been so unfortunate as to disoblige her. That began an intimacy from which the poet probably expected wealth and honours.

And here is Professor Fujimura:

Dennis has left us an amusing account of how Wycherley was accosted in the Mall by the Duchess of Cleveland, after the performance of his first play, and how she thrust herself half out of her coach and complimented him by calling him 'son of a whore', in witty reference to a song in the play.

It does not, you see, take much mental effort to get oneself called 'witty' by Mr. Fujimura. If the Duchess had said something that was *really* witty as well as indecent — say, something like Dr. Johnson's retort to the Thames waterman — we might have been carried along with the argument, but this sort of thing will hardly do.

Before leaving Mr. Fujimura's book, however, we should salute him for having, at any rate, made an onslaught on the very difficult theoretical problems which underlie criticism of this kind of writing, in his chapter 'The Aesthetics of Wit Comedy'. Here such questions as the involvement of moral feelings within an aesthetic experience are, at any rate, posed. Unfortunately one cannot say that Mr. Fujimura comes off best in his brush with them; he keeps catching his foot and sprawling headlong into stuff like:

We do not forget the larger issues of life, nor do we flee them, as Lamb suggested; rather we are so affected by the magic touch of the witty muse that we see such issues in a shimmer of beauty, as when

the first sun-drenched day of spring sets the dewdrops glistening on
the flower tips.

Give me Professor Dobrée.

III

One of the main checks on one's natural wish to take Restoration comedy seriously is, of course, the frightful confusion it
exhibits whenever a moral attitude is to be taken up. Critics who
enthusiastically recommend its fearless questioning of fundamental social questions, or indignantly deny that it is 'immoral',
seldom argue their case with any plausibility. In so far as the charge
of 'immorality' is put in Victorian terms — anything that mentions the unmentionable is immoral — it is easy to brush aside;
but in fact we do expect an artist to have *artistic* morality; to take
up a consistent attitude towards problems of conduct, and not
merely to trifle with them. Trifling is exactly what these dramatists are doing, and their defenders on this score are often driven
to produce desperate arguments. Mr. J. W. Krutch, for instance,
in his *Comedy and Conscience after the Restoration* (1949), has much
to say of comedy but rather less about conscience; he points out
(chap. 2) that there was a lot of corruption in real life at that time,
so the audiences were hardened to it, and adds (p. 39): 'Nor is
there anything in this which need damn the dramatists as men.
They had no deliberate intention of encouraging vice, which,
being men of sense, they no doubt hated.' This will hardly do.
Indeed, Mr. Krutch evidently feels unhappy with it himself,
because, after quoting a few statements by dramatists on the topic
— notably Dryden's Preface to *An Evening's Love* and Mrs.
Behn's Preface to *The Dutch Lover* — he just lets the whole thing
go: 'The truth of the matter seems to be that the poets were not
interested in morality either one way or the other.' A bunch of
footlers, in other words. Mr. J. H. Wilson in his *The Court Wits
of the Restoration* (1948) even takes the view that, since these

writers had no problems to face in their own lives, they had no need to thrash anything out in their work. 'Since their own society was obviously well-ordered, they discussed no problems' (p. 172). It is true that Mr. Wilson — whose book, by the way, is in the main an excellent one — is talking not about Restoration dramatists as a whole, but about a group within them, namely Rochester, Scroope, Etherege, Wycherley, Dorset, Mulgrave, and Buckingham. But he shows no impulse to differentiate between these writers and their socially humbler colleagues. Was the society of Rochester, of Wycherley, of Etherege, so 'obviously well ordered'? Did not these men, in fact, get their lives into a corresponding mess, matching the mess they made of their work?

This talk of getting one's life into a mess reminds me that Rochester, who made one of the most determined of the various efforts to act out these fantasies, and died of it in his thirties, is generally said to be the model for Dorimant in Etherege's *The Man of Mode, or, Sir Fopling Flutter*, and I ought to pause here to say that I except this play from all these remarks about incoherence and indecision. In fact, it is the one play I should feel able to point to, as an example of a Restoration comedy with the courage of its author's convictions. The trouble with the others is that they are simply not facing the real issue, which I take to be a fairly clear-cut one. If a man makes a deliberate choice of a certain way of life, he must know beforehand — or, if he does not, he will very soon find out — that it will bring with it certain special problems. If he decides to play for certain rewards, he will have to encounter certain dangers and penalties. The rakes in Restoration comedy have chosen to live the life of pleasure; they are putting everything into subordination to the satisfaction of their immediate appetites. Now this *could* be the material for a very interesting kind of comedy, one that would include, and make comic play with, the miseries of such a man as well as his delights. But in fact no Restoration comedian took his subject-matter seriously enough to make the attempt: except, as I say, for

Etherege in this one play. Quite apart from its brilliance, *The Man of Mode* is head and shoulders above the other plays of this kind because it is *about* something; Professor Knights's quip, that the play demonstrates nothing 'except the physical stamina of Dorimant', is a mere flippant evasion; its subject is the life-style of a man like Rochester, and its human consequences. Suppose we decide to behave like this, *what will happen*?

Dorimant, in his relationships with women, has the fighter-pilot's mentality; he wants to get them before they get him. He is at war with the sex, and they immediately feel it and feel a very real wish to injure him (which doesn't prevent their feeling attracted to him). When introduced to Harriet, for instance, he begins at once to spar with her in a way that, while superficially it is a mere Beatrice-and-Benedick act to conceal the fact that they have genuine feelings for one another, has within it an element of real malice:

Dorimant. You were talking of Play, Madam; Pray what may be your stint?

Harriet. A little harmless discourse in publick walks, or at most an appointment in a Box bare-fac'd at the Play-House; you are for Masks, and private meetings, where Women engage for all they are worth, I hear.

Dor. I have been us'd to deep Play, but I can make one at small Game, when I like my Gamester well.

Har. And be so unconcern'd you'l ha' no pleasure in't.

Dor. Where there is a considerable sum to be won, the hope of drawing people in, makes every trifle considerable.

Har. The sordidness of mens natures, I know, makes 'em willing to flatter and comply with the Rich, though they are sure never to be the better for 'em.

Dor. 'Tis in their power to do us good, and we despair not but at some time or other they may be willing.

Har. To men who have far'd in this Town like you, 'twould be a great Mortification to live on hope; could you keep a Lent for a Mistriss?

Dor. In expectation of a happy Easter, and though time be very precious, think forty daies well lost, to gain your favour.

Har. Mr. Bellair! let us walk, 'tis time to leave him, men grow dull when they begin to be particular.

Dor. Y'are mistaken, flattery will not ensue, though I know y'are greedy of the praises of the whole Mail.

Har. You do me wrong.

Dor. I do not; as I follow'd you, I observ'd how you were pleased when the *Fops* cry'd *She's handsome, very handsome, by God she is,* and whisper'd aloud your name; the thousand several forms you put your face into; then, to make your self more agreeable, how wantonly you play'd with your head, flung back your locks, and look'd smilingly over your shoulder at 'em.

Har. I do not go begging the mens as you do the Ladies Good liking, with a sly softness in your looks, and a gentle slowness in your bows, as you pass by 'em — as thus, Sir — (*Acts him*) Is not this like you?

After another bout of sparring, later on, Dorimant remarks aside, 'I love her, and dare not let her know it, I fear sh'as an ascendant o're me and may revenge the wrongs I have done her sex.' To make the documentation complete we are shown, earlier on, a typical specimen of these 'wrongs', the truly frightening scene of Dorimant's visit to Mrs. Loveit, the mistress he wishes to be rid of, while she is in the company of Bellinda, whom he has his eye on at the moment; one gets the impression — as, no doubt, one is meant to — that his extreme brutality to Mrs. Loveit is itself a form of sexual display for Bellinda's benefit. Mrs. Loveit, in a fit of agony which has nothing comic about it, tears her fan to pieces:

Dor. Spare your Fan, Madam, you are growing hot, and will want it to cool you.

Lov. Horrour and distraction seize you. Sorrow and Remorse gnaw your Soul, and punish all your Perjuries to me —

(*Weeps.*

Dor. So Thunder breaks the Cloud in Twain,
And makes a passage for the Rain. (*Turning to* Bellinda.
Bellinda, you are the Devil that have rais'd this storm;

(*To* Bellinda.

you were at the Play yesterday, and have been making discoveries
to your Dear.

Bell. Y'are the most mistaken Man i' the World.

Dor. It must be so, and here I vow revenge; resolve to pursue, and
persecute you more impertinently than ever any Loving Fop did
his Mistress, hunt you i' the *Park*, trace you i' the *Mail*, dog you in
every visit you make, haunt you at the Plays, and i' the Drawing
Room, hang my nose in your neck, and talk to you whether you
will or no, and ever look upon you with such dying Eyes, till
your Friends grow Jealous of me, send you out of Town, and the
World suspect your reputation.

(In a lower voice

At my Lady *Townley's* when we go from hence.

(He looks kindly on Bellinda.

Bell. I'le meet you there.

Goaded by this, Mrs. Loveit launches herself across the room
and tries to push him away, crying, 'Stand off, you sha'not stare
upon her so.' On Dorimant's retorting (significantly), 'Good!
There's one made jealous already,' the poor creature is reduced to
playing a card that she knows will be useless, but cannot help
producing:

Loveit. Is this the constancy you vow'd?

Dor. Constancy at my years! 'tis not a Virtue in season, you might
as well expect the Fruit the Autumn ripens i' the Spring . . . Youth
has a long Journey to go, Madam; should I have set up my rest at
the first Inn I lodg'd at, I should never have arriv'd at the happiness
I now enjoy.

The old commonplace of Restoration comedy is trotted out,
but this time it rings true because we are shown the consequences,
among them the uneasiness that preys on Dorimant. Throughout
the play he is shown as barely managing to hold his own, and in
one scene the women definitely get the better of him and humiliate
him without mercy (Act V, Sc. i). All in all, the reader or spectator of the play is left in no doubt as to the nature of the sexual
relationship that is its main subject-matter; each side is lusting for
the other's downfall and suffering. Dorimant is seriously annoyed

when Mrs. Loveit manages to regain her composure and draw
some sort of a veil over her feelings for him; savagely he promises
himself to put an end to all that: 'had it not been for some powerful Considerations which will be removed tomorrow morning, I
had made her pluck off the mask, and shew the passion that lyes
panting under'.

One can, in fact, comfortably discuss this play without men-
tioning its eponym, though a complete account would have, of
course, to make due mention of Sir Fopling as a satisfactory
'brilliant' piece of satiric portraiture. But the centre of the play is
Dorimant's warfare against women, whom he takes on in the persons of Mrs. Loveit, Harriet, and Bellinda. The ruthlessness of
Etherege's logic makes the play harrowing, but at least it is never
false and unsatisfactory; it is literature, where most other Restoration comedy is mere diversion, on however high a level. The
ending, whereby Harriet is left in (temporary?) possession of
Dorimant's affections, is free of the usual sentimentality; he is
going down to the country to court her, in what she describes
as:

> a great rambling lone house, that looks as it were not inhabited, the
> family's so small; there you'l find my Mother, an old lame Aunt, and
> my self, Sir, perch'd up on Chairs at a distance in a large parlour;
> sitting moping like three or four Melancholy Birds in a spacious
> vollary — Does not this stagger your Resolution?

Harriet can trade badinage with Dorimant amiably enough,
considering the ferocity with which she has got rid of all com-
petition. A moment before uttering these lines, for instance, she
has turned to the grief-stricken Loveit with: 'Mr. *Dorimant* has
been your God Almighty long enough, 'tis time to think of
another.'

The ruthlessness of all these people, though unpleasant to read
about, has at least the harsh ring of truth; when men like Dorimant are tamed, it is generally by pert baggages like Harriet who

have the necessary savagery. But, though I cannot claim to have read the whole corpus, I am fairly sure there is nothing else in Restoration comedy that carries this kind of conviction.

Wycherley, at any rate, never achieved clarity on any basic moral issue. The whole plot of the *Plain Dealer* is simply a piece of crude misanthropy and getting one's own back. No doubt it is rather a neat trick, when a mistress has deceived and deserted you, to enjoy her in a darkened room when she thinks you are somebody else; and if, at the end of the play, you can get the love of a good woman and a handsome lump sum in addition, surely that *proves* you are the hero of the piece. If Wycherley's mind really worked like this, he must have been little better than an idiot, and a nasty idiot into the bargain. *The Country Wife* is even worse, because more tangled. Horner is meant to be admired for his clever trick, but Harcourt is equally so for his persistent attempt to marry Alithea honourably. It is the same with Congreve. Most of *Love for Love* is in fact pretty direct propaganda *for* good sexual morality; one notes the conversion of Scandal, and the punishment of Tattle, which is rather like that of Lucio in *Measure for Measure*. At first sight it looks as if Congreve were in favour of a simple 'wild oats' outlook, where the characters settle down to marriage after a period on the tiles. But there is a harshness that goes uncomfortably with any such genial tolerance. What about Valentine's illegitimate son? Is he to get any share in the warmth and affection that is being slopped about in the last scene? Admittedly it is trying to be dunned for money, but Valentine's reaction to being told of the arrival of 'the Nurse with one of your Children from *Twitnam*' is a little harsh, even in the circumstances:

> Pox on her, cou'd she find no other time to fling my Sins in my Face: Here, give her this [*Gives Mony.*] and bid her trouble me no more; a thoughtless two handed Whore, she knows my Condition well enough, and might have overlaid the Child a Fortnight ago, if she had had any forecast in her.

No doubt we are to think he does not mean this seriously, as his friend Scandal refers to the boy as 'my Godson'; but, considering that the whole thing is only brought in by way of stage patter, it seems an odd way of getting a laugh.

Mirabell is another case. In *The Way of the World*, Congreve brought Restoration comedy up to the very frontiers of respectability; except for his much greater brilliance, he all but joins hands with Goldsmith and Sheridan. But in their haste to approve of Mirabell as much as they do of Charles Surface, some critics have simply not noticed what a cad he is. Hear Professor Fujimura giving him a character:

> Mrs. Fainall, we gather, was an attachment of the past, before he fell in love; and since she was a widow at the time, and hence, according to the naturalistic conception of widows, highly inflammable, he could hardly be blamed for satisfying her sexual appetite as well as his own. When the play opens, Mirabell has apparently broken off all relations with her, and he is pursuing matrimony with a serious purpose.

Not a word about the fact that he has pushed Mrs. Fainall into a marriage of hell, to suit his own convenience; indeed he tells her in so many words that it was in case she became pregnant: when she rounds on him with, 'Why did you make me marry this Man?' he answers airily, 'Why do we daily commit disagreeable and dangerous Actions? To save that Idol Reputation. If the Familiarities of our Loves had produc'd that Consequence, of which you were apprehensive, where cou'd you have fix'd a Father's Name with Credit, but on a Husband?' Admirable realism, no doubt, but this man is the *hero*; we are supposed to care whether he is happy or not; no wonder Lamb could only defend these plays by saying that they were simply aesthetic patterns with no humanity involved at all.

These strictures could perhaps be met by the counter-accusation that I am asking for a neat black-and-white pattern, with the good people rewarded and the bad ones punished. If Manly behaves like a cad, and still comes out on top, why not? That's life, isn't it? I see this objection, yet the whole nature of these plays forbids my admitting it. Quite apart from the fact that in comedy, the good people *are* usually rewarded and the bad ones discomfited — it is this, more than any other single feature, that stamps it as comedy — these plays are not comedies merely but satiric comedies; their writers are always claiming that they are out to pillory vice and folly 'with an armed and resolved hand'. Manly is not a portrait of a cad who exploits his caddishness and gets away with it; he is meant to be a pattern of surly virtue, and his tiresome parade of moral superiority, though cant, is unconscious cant. There have been, it is true, examples of writers who broke clear of the conventions they set out to observe; Wycherley might be defended as an author who goes beyond the usual scope of moralistic comedy and produces a new kind, a problem-play made out of comic ingredients. But though I can imagine such an argument, I cannot make this claim; I must leave it for someone else to do; the notion of the Restoration comedians as writers of Shavian debates on moral and social issues — in my opinion, it simply does not hold water. I should prefer to rest the defence mainly on a humbler argument; that these dramatists are saved by their incidental excellences, notably their spirited drawing of grotesques. If, on mature consideration, we decided that their works were deformed wholes, rendered tolerable by the brilliance of isolated parts, should we be surprised? Would it be the first time we had come across such works?

What, after all — to put the question another way — are the most *enjoyable* passages in Wycherley and Congreve? — the passages we should point to if we wanted to convince a doubter that he would find some pleasure in their plays if he read them over, or went to see them? To my mind, the answer is clear; not the smart-Alec 'combats of wit', not the vaunted 'social criticism', but the passages which have some richness of language; and this means, in practice, their passages of broad comedy, when the buffoons take the stage. The only time when these dramatists write like poets, when any kind of colour and life radiate from the words on the page, is when they are writing speeches for their grotesques to utter. In these scenes they are the heirs of Shakespeare. It hardly needs to be argued that these writers were conscious of Shakespeare; his achievement was tangibly present to their minds, so that they were forever introducing random scraps of his material into their work; what I am arguing here is that their best moments nearly always come when they are imitating Shakespeare's trick of getting a grotesque, but rich, comic effect by means of language alone. One of the ways in which Shakespeare proved himself a great poet was by his gift of spinning out yards of material from an empty top-hat; some of his best comic writing is based on the flimsiest and stalest of jokes, and the result is a virtuoso exercise, as if he had been challenged to write well on third-rate music-hall material. Take, for example, Bardolph's red nose, which, as Dr. Johnson severely remarked, 'seems to have taken more hold on Shakespeare's imagination than any other'. This is true; Shakespeare was the only one who thought it funny; yet he lavishes resources on it that boost the subject up to many times its natural power. Most of us, I take it, would sacrifice any ten pages of the 'serious' writing in *Henry IV, Part I*, rather than let go a passage like this one:

Bard. Why, Sir *Iohn*, my Face does you no harme.
Falst. No, Ile be sworne: I make as good vse of it, as many a man doth of a Deaths-Head, or a *Memento Mori*. I neuer see thy Face, but I thinke vpon Hell fire, and *Diues* that liued in Purple; for there he is in his Robes burning, burning. If thou wert any way giuen to vertue, I would sweare by thy Face; my Oath should bee, *By this Fire*, that's God's Angel.[1] But thou art altogether giuen ouer; and wert indeede, but for the Light in thy Face, the Sunne of vtter Darkenesse. When thou ran'st vp Gads-Hill in the Night, to catch my Horse, if I did not thinke that thou hadst beene an *Ignis fatuus*, or a Ball of Wild-fire, there's no Purchase in Money. O

[1] Reading of Quartos 3 to 8.

thou art a perpetuall Triumph, an euerlasting Bone-fire-Light:
thou hast saued me a thousand Markes in Linkes and Torches,
walking with thee in the Night betwixt Tauerne and Tauerne:
but the Sack that thou hast drunke me, would haue bought me
Lights as good cheape, as the dearest chandlers in Europe. I haue
maintain'd that Salamander of yours with fire, any time this two
and thirtie yeeres, Heauen reward me for it.

Bard. I would my Face were in your Belly.

Falst. So should I be sure to be heart-burn'd.

The trick is to keep the thing going without anything to back
it up except language. Congreve and Wycherley can both do this,
and if we want proof that these men were poets, we shall find it
here much more readily than in their 'official' versifications. (The
only Restoration 'wit' who was a genuine poet *in verse* was
Rochester, to my mind.) When I say that Wycherley and Congreve 'imitated' Shakespeare in this respect, I may be putting it
too specifically; but at all events they showed, when they
attempted this kind of thing, that they had inherited a splinter of
Shakespeare's sensibility. Congreve has the best examples, and the
most frequent; the reason being, obviously, that he is on the whole
the best stylist. So there is no need for quotation to establish the
point about *him*. But Wycherley has it too. Take the sort of lines
he writes for the Widow Blackacre. She has been approached
(*The Plain Dealer*, II, i) by two suitors, an old man and a young
one. I will not copy out the interruptions, cries of 'How, lady!'
and 'Hey, brave mother', etc., but just give her lines.

'First, I say, for you, Major, my walking Hospital of an ancient
Foundation, thou Bag of Mummy, that wouldst fall asunder, if
'twere not for thy Cere-cloaths —

'Thou wither'd hobling, distorted Cripple; nay, thou art a
Cripple all over; wou'dst thou make me the Staff of thy Age, the
Crutch of thy Decrepidness? Me —

'Thou senseless, impertinent, quibling, driveling, feeble, para-
lytick, impotent, fumbling, frigid Nincompoop!

'Wou'dst thou make a Caudlemaker, a Nurse of me? Can't you be

Bed-rid without a Bed-fellow? Won't your Swan-skins, Furrs, Flannels, and the scorch'd Trencher keep you warm there? Wou'd you have me your Scotch Warming-pan, with a pox to you? Me! —

'If I wou'd have marry'd an old Man, 'tis well known I might have marry'd an Earl; nay, what's more, a Judge, and been covered the Winter-nights with the Lamb-skins, which I prefer to the Ermins of Nobles: And durst thou think I wou'd wrong my poor Minor, there, for you?'

The young suitor, for his part, gets, among other things, this broadside:

Freeman. Nay, prythee, Widow hear me.
Widow. No, Sir, I'd have you to know, thou pitiful, paltry, lath-back'd Fellow, if I wou'd have marry'd a young Man, 'tis well known, I cou'd have had any young Heir in *Norfolk*; nay, the hopefull'st young Man this day at the *King's-Bench Bar*; I, that am a Relict and Executrix of known plentiful assets and parts, who understand my self and the Law: And wou'd you have me under Covert-Baron again? No, Sir, no Covert Baron for me.

Some readers will exclaim, Jonson! But although this passage, with its smattering of law-terms, is Jonsonian in its method — Jonson liked to read up bits of specialist information and then throw them into his comic tirades, as in *The Alchemist* — I fancy the real impulse towards this kind of thing is Shakespearean, so far as it derived from a literary source at all. After all, Shakespeare played this game better than anyone else, and they would naturally follow the most conspicuous leader, however much they talked of 'humours'. Dryden is on my side here; his famous verse compliment to Congreve, on *The Old Batchelor*, says he is like Shakespeare, and I do not believe this is just large and meaningless talk.

It would take too long to list all, or most, of the Shakespearean echoes in Wycherley and Congreve, but I believe anyone who knows his Shakespeare fairly thoroughly will be pulled up every two or three pages by something that is unmistakably lifted. Sometimes it will be a verbal echo, sometimes a situation. Fidelia, in *The Plain Dealer*, might be paralleled in many Elizabethan plays, but one feels that the model for any beautiful and virtuous girl masquerading as a boy, in English drama, is basically Shake-spearean. Elsewhere in the play, fragments of Shakespeare come through in a distorted way; the widow Blackacre's comic grief about 'my child and my writings' gets a laugh by the same device as Shylock's 'my daughter and my ducats'; Vernish, the false friend, says of Manly, 'I'll lead the easy, honest fool by the nose', which is a direct verbal reminiscence of one of Iago's speeches; Manly, invited to 'dine with my lord', retorts 'No, no; the ordinary is too dear for me, where flattery must pay for my dinner,' which has the ring of Enobarbus's account of Antony at Cleopatra's dinner-party — 'And for his ordinary, paies his heart, For what his eyes eate onely.' *Othello* and *Hamlet* were, on the whole, the two plays that obsessed these dramatists; one never reads far without coming across something that recalls one or the other. Wycherley, though a clumsy writer and unable even to imitate another man's rhythms successfully (in some respects this is to his credit, of course), even gives Manly's lines a breath, now and then, of the bitter melancholy of Hamlet's prose speeches.

In Congreve's case it is the same; I shall give no details, since it is so obvious as to be boring. The reader who wants to see what I mean in a hurry, without bothering to work through the plays, might turn to the scenes in *The Double Dealer* where Maskwell is working up Lord Touchwood's suspicions of his wife (the reminiscence of *Othello* even extends to making the victim cry out 'give me the Occular Proof!'), and, of course, Valentine's ravings when he is feigning madness, in *Love for Love*. Charles Whibley presumably thought he was praising Congreve when he said that Valentine 'speaks in the very accent of Hamlet', but I am afraid it is more to the point to say, simply, that Congreve's writing in these scenes is embarrassingly tied to Shakespeare's, in spite of his efforts to break free. Nor is it, of course, only Congreve and Wycherley who are under this compulsion; all the Restoration dramatists share it, so that in reading their work we soon learn to watch for the lumps of undigested Bard; merely sighing wearily as we note, for instance, that the Nurse in Vanbrugh's *The Relapse* is a tenth-rate copy of the Nurse in *Romeo and Juliet*.

IV

But if these dramatists are obsessed by Shakespeare, there is one important respect in which they take a pride in not resembling him or any other Elizabethan. In the comedies of Shakespeare's age it was customary to have two relatively simple plots; in Restoration comedy it is *de rigueur* to bind everything up into a single very complicated one. The motive is, in each case, clear enough; the Elizabethan double plot helped the play to deal with a wider sweep of life; Restoration dramatists thought it vulgar to deal with a wide sweep of life, and in any case were hampered by a notion of elegance which, inexplicably, forbade multiple plots while countenancing absurd constrictions and convolutions within the single plot.

In fact, the plots of Restoration comedies are usually the worst thing about them. To recount, baldly, the action of half a dozen of these plays is to be left with an appalling sense of futility. Even Shakespeare's comic structures have more interest — and, in any case, the merit of Shakespearean comedy is, like that of the Dickensian novel, slightly to one side of the actual plot; it consists in the creation of a world. In Restoration comedy the plot is placed rather centrally; it is one of the things we are meant to admire; it also makes a show of dealing directly with the material of daily life — a heightened and smoothed-out version of the daily life of the fashionable set in the audience. Money, for instance, is a constant theme, whereas Shakespeare hardly ever mentions it in his 'golden' comedies (I don't mean things like Shylock's five thousand ducats). These plots make a show of realism, which they at once destroy by turning into fantastic arabesques: it is one more symptom of the narrowing process that can be seen

going on all through the seventeenth century. They withdrew
their sympathies into a limited area, and then proceeded to weave
intricate patterns within that area. It is something to do with the
civilization they were living in, of course; it is like the difference
between Byrd and Purcell; but if we trace the process through
music alone we get too flattering a view of it. This stately
formality, which delights in patterns, is not really well served by
fribbling ingenuity. Compare the dances which Purcell wrote for
The Old Batchelor with the play itself! Or, if I seemed a moment
ago to be over-kind to Shakespeare's comic plots, compare the
most outrageous of them with the plot of *The Way of the World*,
which, since I cannot sort it out myself, I give in the words of
Mr. Crane Taylor:

> Mirabell is in love with Millamant, niece and ward of Lady Wish-
> fort, who intends that she shall marry her nephew Sir Wilfull Wit-
> woud, a country squire. In order to disguise his love for Millamant,
> Mirabell affects a fondness for Lady Wishfort, who discovers his
> duplicity and is highly incensed. When cajolery fails to win her
> favour, Mirabell plays a prank on her which, if publicly known,
> would make her the laughing-stock of the town. To secure complete
> secrecy and safeguard Lady Wishfort, he has his man Waitwell
> marry her maid Foible, and then court Lady Wishfort in the guise of
> Sir Rowland. Mrs. Marwood, jealous of Mirabell's love for Milla-
> mant, had previously disclosed his false pretences to Lady Wishfort,
> and now informs her of this trick also. Fainall, a rakish acquaintance
> of Mirabell, married Lady Wishfort's daughter, formerly a mistress
> of Mirabell, in order to secure her fortune. Mrs. Marwood, Fainall's
> mistress, advises him that he may secure all of Lady Wishfort's
> fortune, including the amount held in trust for Millamant, by
> threatening to expose her daughter, his wife, as an immoral charac-
> ter. As he is making his accusation before the assembled characters,
> Mincing and Foible, maids to Millamant and Lady Wishfort, give
> evidence of the relation between Mrs. Marwood and Fainall. He is
> enraged, and swears to publish his wife's scandal if her fortune is not
> assigned to him. Mirabell offers to help Lady Wishfort out of this
> dilemma, and she promises him her niece Millamant. Thereupon, he
> produces a will, sworn to by Witwoud and Petulant, two fops who

could write their names but read little; this will was made by Lady
Wishfort's daughter before she married Fainall, and conveys all of
her property in trust to her friend Mirabell. Thus, she and Lady
Wishfort are safeguarded, Fainall and Mrs. Marwood are thwarted,
and Mirabel and Millamant are to be married.

One can only say, faced with this kind of thing, that there seems
to be a kind of cross-word puzzle pleasure for which most people
have a streak of hankering, and that this pleasure wanders about,
so to speak, and attaches itself, in a parasitic way, to this or that
'host' among the arts. In our time, complicated plots have gone
out (except on the pictures, where they baffle highbrows much
more than the rest of the audience), and puzzle-interest has
attached itself to poetry. This is, at any rate, the only defence of
such a plot that occurs to me.

It is, to repeat the word, a *narrowing*. Shakespeare could see that
his 'low-life' characters were funny, but at the same time he was
able to identify with them to some extent; Dogberry is a butt, no
doubt, and yet he is still an officer of the watch, and he is given an
important part in the action. This, as well as being true to life
('odd people, whom you would normally laugh at, can sometimes put you in their debt'), gives the play a richness of effect
that comes through as a kind of glow. It is like holding a glass of
wine up to the light; if you hold Restoration comedy up to the
light, you see no glow; the glass is simply lined with paper of the
right colour. To take a familiar example — everything in Shakespeare is familiar, by this time — we might select Dogberry's
gobbling with outraged dignity as he arrests the villains.

> Dost thou not suspect my place? does thou not suspect my yeeres?
> O that hee were heere to write mee downe an asse! but masters,
> remember that I am an asse: though it be not written down, yet
> forget not that I am an asse: No thou villaine, thou art full of piety
> as shall be prou'd vpon thee by good witnesse, I am a wise fellow,
> and which is more, an officer, and which is more, a houshoulder, and
> which is more, as pretty a peece of flesh as any in Messina, and one
> that knowes the Law, goe to, and a rich fellow enough, goe to, and a

fellow that hath had losses, and one that hath two gownes, and euery thing handsome about him: bring him away: O that I had been writ downe an asse!

What were the *losses*, we wonder? Did he get fleeced of some of his money, or is it an intimate, personal loss? The mere fact that we can speculate is the important point; Shakespeare has drawn in a dimension behind Dogberry, giving him, in that one phrase, a history and an identity. The reason why this kind of thing is so rare in Restoration comedy is not because they were incapable of it; it is not a very uncommon achievement, though naturally Shakespeare is better at it than everyone else (he is better at *anything* than everyone else). It is because of the narrowing, the withdrawal of sympathies. Everything is seen from the point of view of one class, and of one type of person within that class. There are passages in Wycherley and Congreve where the comic character becomes a real person, but they stick out more obviously as exceptions; they are like tapers which barely get alight before they flicker out in the harsher atmosphere. Wycherley's chief example, I suppose, is the Country Wife herself, and particularly the one quotation that everyone knows — the half-pathetic little postscript to one of her letters to Horner: 'Be sure you love me, whatever my husband says to the contrary, and let him not see this, lest he should come home and pinch me, or kill my squirrel.'

Congreve, a more perceptive and, on the whole, better-hearted man than Wycherley, has more of this quality. I find a distinct flavour of it in the scene where Sir Sampson Legend is momentarily fooled into thinking that Angelica will really marry him (*Love for Love*, V, ii). She, in the approved heartless manner, has her own motives for leading him by the nose. The result might have been something like the terrible 'Nacky, Nacky' scene in *Venice Preserv'd*; indeed Congreve cannot be accused of failing to pour appropriate scorn on that favourite butt of the time, the lustful dotard; but Sir Sampson comes out of it, after all, not wholly disgraced. Of course he was the right social class, which must have been a help.

It is clear, in any case, that Sir Sampson is one of the characters whose lines Congreve most enjoyed writing; in the priggish letter to Dennis in which he tried to express the *rationale* of his work, he harked back to the Jonsonian 'humour', and no doubt the old man is a prime specimen: but the real motive for creating him was to use up some of the fund of exuberantly comic language that Congreve was so good at spouting. The exchange between him and Foresight (II, v) is very lovingly written, and shall be quoted.

> Sir Samp. . . . Pox o'th' time; there's no time but the time present, there's no more to be said of what's past, and all that is to come will happen. If the Sun shine by Day, and the Stars by Night, why, we shall know one another's Faces without the help of a Candle, and that's all the Stars are good for.
>
> Fore. How, how? Sir *Sampson*, that all? Give me leave to contradict you, and tell you, you are ignorant.
>
> Sir Samp. I tell you, I am wise; and *sapiens dominabitur astris*; there's Latin for you to prove it, and an Argument to confound your *Ephemeris* — Ignorant! — I tell you, I have travell'd old *Fircu*, and know the Globe. I have seen the *Antipodes*, where the Sun rises at Midnight, and sets at Noon-Day.
>
> Fore. But I tell you, I have travell'd, and travell'd in the Coelestial *Spheres*, known the *Signs* and the *Planets*, and their Houses. Can judge of Motions Direct and Retrograde, of *Sextiles*, *Quadrates*, *Trines* and *Oppositions*, Fiery *Trigons* and Aquatical *Trigons*. Know whether Life shall be long or short, Happy or Unhappy, whether Diseases are Curable or Incurable. If Journeys shall be prosperous, Undertakings successful; or Goods Stoll'n recover'd, I know —
>
> Sir Samp. I know the length of the Emperor of *China*'s Foot; have kiss'd the *Great Mogul*'s Slipper, and rid a Hunting upon an Elephant with the Cham of *Tartary*, — Body o'me, I have made a Cuckold of a King, and the present Majesty of *Bantam* is the Issue of these Loins.
>
> Fore. I know when Travellers lye or speak Truth, when they don't know it themselves.

Sir Samp. I have known an Astrologer made a Cuckold in the Twinkling of a Star; and seen a Conjuror that cou'd not keep the Devil out of his Wife's Circle.

Fore. What, does he twit me with my Wife too? I must be better inform'd of them, — *Aside.* — Do you mean my Wife, Sir *Sampson*? Tho' you made a Cuckold of the King of *Bantam*, yet by the Body of the Sun —

Sir Samp. By the Horns of the Moon, you wou'd say, Brother *Capricorn*.

Fore. Capricorn in your Teeth, thou Modern *Mandevil*; *Ferdinand Mendez Pinto* was but a Type of thee, thou Liar of the first Magnitude. Take back your Paper of Inheritance; send your Son to Sea again. I'll wed my Daughter to an *Egyptian* Mummy, e'er she shall Incorporate with a Contemner of Sciences, and a Defamer of Virtue.

Sir Samp. Body o'me, I have gone too far; — I must not provoke honest *Albumazar*, — an *Egyptian* Mummy is an Illustrious Creature, my trusty Hieroglyphick; and may have Significations of Futurity about him; Odsbud, I would my Son were an *Egyptian* Mummy for thy sake. What, thou art not angry for a Jest, my good *Haly* — I reverence the Sun, Moon and Stars with all my Heart. — What, I'll make thee a Present of a Mummy: Now I think on't, Body o'me, I have a Shoulder of an *Egyptian* King, that I purloin'd from one of the Pyramids, powder'd with Hieroglyphicks, thou shalt have it brought home to thy House, and make an Entertainment for all the *Philomaths*, and Students in Physick and Astrology in and about *London*.

Fore. But what do you know of my Wife, Sir *Sampson*?

Sir Samp. Thy Wife is a Constellation of Virtues; she's the Moon, and thou art the Man in the Moon: Nay, she is more Illustrious than the Moon; for she has her Chastity without her Inconstancy, s'bud I was but in Jest.

The vaunted 'social criticism', then, is nothing; the vaunted 'wit', not much; the broad comedy is what mainly carries these plays along; this puts these writers in alignment with, let us say, Fielding and the early Dickens, rather than with the fine discriminators and the delicate ironists. If I have made this point clearly enough, it is almost time for me to stop: but there is one more point still to make. Wycherley and Congreve ought to be given their due. If the false praise is finally disposed of, let us not empty away the true praise with it. In fact I want to end with something not far off a *volte-face*.

Throughout this essay I have been talking as if confusion were always and everywhere a bad thing, by comparison with clarity. I have denied these dramatists the status of acute social commentators, even the status of serious artists, because their work is riddled with inconsistencies; because they make fun of marriage, for instance, for five long acts and then meekly lead the hero to the altar in the last scene. Why (I have been asking) should we be asked to admire both Horner and Harcourt in the same play? If Fidelia Grey is a 'good' character, why is not Manly a bad one?

Up to a point, I think this argument holds. A writer cannot very well obtain our assent, intellectual or emotional, if he is in an utter muddle over the fundamentals of what he is talking about. On the other hand, it is something if he succeeds in documenting, in a convincing and memorable way, a confusion that exists in the society he lives in. He might even be said to make it his aim, whether consciously or not, to demonstrate and exploit this confusion. I think we should give over all attempt to build up the Restoration dramatists as inquiring minds, keenly watching the social seismograph, and think of them rather as minor but genuine artists whose great merit is that they were sensitive to the dominant confusions of their epoch, and able to render them in all their richness. Most of these confusions existed around the topic of sexual morality, and marriage in particular. And here we may notice a clue; marital infidelity is taken almost for granted — as it has to be if the comic plot is to get started at all — but *marriage is regarded as indissoluble*. Two or three times in the mass of Restoration comedy one might come across a mention of divorce, but generally speaking it is simply not taken into account. It follows that the attitude to marriage that we find in these plays is the same, broadly speaking — and allowing for comic exaggeration

— as that taken in any society where marriage is indissoluble. Today, if we want jokes in the comic papers about cuckoldry, the place to look for them is in the Latin countries, where divorce is either not allowed for by the law, or purposely made difficult and expensive. The Nordic, Protestant kind of society, which is trying to proceed on the assumption that an unhappy marriage is better washed out, tends not to see anything funny in the 'hang-your-hat-on-his-horns' *motif*.

It is a matter of common sense that once divorce is socially recognized there will be a falling-off in trench humour about marriage. Only people who regard marriage as a once-and-for-all plunge, and hence as a desperately dangerous adventure, will be able to joke about it in this way. Their attitude is in itself illogical; it is illogical to take something so seriously that you leave yourself no way of commenting on it except by ribaldry; but it happens to be the attitude that most human beings, even now, adopt. If we look at Restoration comedy as literature, rather than as a narrowly social document, we shall see that what it really demonstrates is the invincible strength of the institution of marriage. The comic resentment ('Why should a foolish marriage vow That long ago was made', etc.) is the nearest they dare get to a radical criticism of it; their most destructive comment on marriage is to point out that people are sometimes unfaithful to one another, which is about the same as saying that glass is unsuitable for making windows with because it sometimes gets broken. It is significant that the real onslaught on marriage, in the lifetime of these men, was made by someone who had less sense of humour, and less belief in the therapeutic value of a good laugh, than they had; Milton, who was the diametric opposite of a man like Wycherley, spent years campaigning vehemently for divorce on the grounds of incompatibility; the Restoration dramatists would be no more likely to do this than they would be to write religious epic poems. They were, like all jokers, men of compromise; their theme was the moulding of human nature to fit in with 'the armies of unalterable law', where Milton's attitude was that these things should be met head-on; Samson pulling down the temple of Dagon was his ideal of behaviour, and it is not a comic one.

I do not think, then, that the Restoration comedians should be dismissed on the grounds that they were inconsistent and muddled, though earlier on I had to argue as if I did think so, if only to dispel the clouds of incense. Realistic writers have to reflect what actually goes on, and it is a fact that most people not only never achieve, but never try for, the kind of clarity that makes them take up a consistent attitude towards the bedrock facts of their lives. Restoration comedy shows us a world in which people put up with — on the whole, gladly enough — a set of confusions remarkably like our own; they managed, as we manage, to rub along with them somehow; they had no very effective way of dealing with serious problems, except to laugh at them, but in this again they were much like ourselves. Congreve and Wycherley were not great writers, and the rest (setting aside Etherege as the author of one remarkable play) are not even worth considering as artists; but their work has lived, and I suspect that the reason for this is that they had the comedian's gift of not pressing for a logical solution, but accepting the muddle and making it seem, for all their artificiality, genuinely human.

(1955)

OVID IN ENGLISH

People may say what they like of the inadequacy of translation, it is and it remains one of the weightiest and worthiest of employments in the general life of the world. — Goethe

L'oeuvre dure en tant qu'elle est capable de paraître tout autre que son auteur l'avait faite. — Paul Valéry

The old versions of Ovid are worth more than a week's random reading. — Ezra Pound

EVERYONE with an interest in English literature, at any rate before the nineteenth century, has sooner or later to get on to terms with Ovid. But if you don't already know Latin, it seems uneconomical to learn it just for his sake; most literary people know *some* Latin, but not enough to make it anything better than drudgery to read through so voluminous a poet as Ovid from end to end. And so we come, as usual, to the point where we begin to look round for 'the translations'. What translations? There are, of course, plenty; there is the Loeb; the *Metamorphoses* are in the Penguin Classics, and have also been put into verse by an American poet, Rolfe Humphries; and so on. But since most people's interest in Ovid is, in fact, dictated by his strategic importance in classical English literature (Shakespeare's favourite poet, etc., etc.), it seems reasonable to look at the translations that were made during Ovid's reign, during the time when he was the most-loved Latin poet among us. One has heard tell that these translations are famous poems in their own right; Sandys, and Golding, and Marlowe, and Dryden have struck poetry from Ovid that has stayed alive on its own. And so one turns to them, with the object, at first, of merely assimilating a little Ovid the easy way.

It proves, however, to be more complicated and at the same time much more interesting than we expected. We find ourselves getting side-tracked, but without minding, because the side-tracks are interesting; the obvious affection that all these men felt for Ovid becomes something real, something we want to know more about. Turning for help to the specialist scholars, one finds that even they, who know so frighteningly much, are only feeling their way among these very tricky questions.

I have long thought that one of the most useful books that could be put together, in some don's spare time, would be a *composite* translation of Ovid's works into English; a few pages from one translator, a few from another, moving from one period to the next; it would bring out the colours and shapes of English literary history like nothing else. And it would be fairly easy. I hope someone will do it. The object of this essay is partly to make a plea for the compilation of such a book, and partly just to air the topics most immediately connected with the name of Ovid in an English setting.

My starting-point is that, whether we like it or not, a classical training is no longer the normal equipment of an educated man or woman. The place occupied during the last three centuries by the poetry, oratory, and philosophy of Greece and Rome (the first usually filtered through the second) has now been, largely, usurped by the literature of our own tongue. A speaker in the House of Commons who, a century ago, would have quoted Horace or Virgil to illustrate or clinch his argument will nowadays go no further than Shakespeare: he would, in fact, simply irritate his hearers by quoting in Latin, a language which they are no longer obliged to pretend to follow.

'The murder of classical education', a modern sage has remarked, 'was an inside job'; and it may be, perhaps, that this decline can be laid at the door of the teachers to whom the subject was entrusted during the middle and late nineteenth century, when more and more knowledge was being made available by 'research', and the bringing of an appreciation of Latin and Greek to a correspondingly wider public was, somehow, always somebody else's job. It is not for an outsider, one of the casualties in this defeat, to pass judgement; but even an outsider can see the force of Professor Highet's comment:

The belief that the study and teaching of classical literatures ought to be purely and scientifically objective has spoilt many a teacher and many, many good pupils. It was largely responsible for the recession in public interest in the classics during the latter half of the nineteenth century. Put broadly, it has meant that classical scholars feel more obliged to extend knowledge than to disseminate it. The gap between the scholar and the public, which in the Renaissance and in the revolutionary era was bridged by a constant interflow of teaching and questioning and propaganda and imitation and translation and emulation, has been widened to a gulf. (*The Classical Tradition*, 1949, cap. XXI.)

And so the responsibility for introducing each new generation to the elements of civilization has passed to 'English' — which itself is in danger of following the example of classical studies by narrowing its field of interest to the trivial and the *recherché*. At all events, there has come into existence a large body of readers who are on close terms with the principal English poets since Chaucer, while of the classical authors to whom these poets devoted years of loving attention, they are wholly or partly ignorant. What, briefly, are such readers missing?

To begin with, they are missing the stylistic echoes. A line in Milton or Tennyson which the author shaped in unconscious, or delightedly conscious, imitation of a line of Virgil, is to them just another line, which has to be taken simply on its merits as English poetry. Commentators can point out these echoes, but it is unlikely that their learning will benefit anyone except other commentators. About this, therefore, there is little or nothing to be done, and it is no use worrying too much about it. Mark Pattison assured his audience that an appreciation of Milton was 'the last reward of consummate scholarship', and he may have been right; but the corollary, that unless you are a consummate scholar it is better to leave Milton alone, is obviously false.

A far more important, because far more crippling, loss is the fact that fewer and fewer people have any idea of what classical literature is *about*. It is quite common to meet people who, though

they had to read at least two books of the *Aeneid* at school, have
only the vaguest idea of the story of the whole poem, and could
certainly not summarize it correctly and put the episodes in the
right order; and if this is true of Virgil, how much more true
must it be of the less widely prescribed authors? The 'Miss
Bertrams' in *Mansfield Park* learnt 'a great deal of heathen
mythology', as naturally as they learnt 'the chronological order of
the kings of England, with the dates of their accession, and most
of the principal events of their reigns', but that time, unhappily
for literature, is over. The result is that it is increasingly difficult
for a poet to make use of classical mythology as symbol or
illustration, and that the great poets of the past, who introduced it
without hesitation and (often) without stint, have to be paraded
with strings of footnotes, like halters, about their necks. For,
although the spirit of pagan literature has been variously inter-
preted in various ages, its matter has been directly and con-
tinuously absorbed into English literature, so that few people
would seriously disagree with the findings of Mr. C. S. Lewis:

> You can read English poetry for days on end without coming
> across classic form or classic feeling; but you will have been inundated
> with references to how Acteon died or what birds saved the Capitol,
> what Agesilaus said or Pompey did, the constitution of Sparta, the
> matrimonial troubles of Socrates, and some one's witty reply to
> Alexander. It is this kind of influence that lies on the surface of our
> literature and meets every one's gaze; and it is of this that most
> people are really thinking when they say that our origins are in
> Greece and Rome.

Assuming, then, that while it is no longer possible to aim at a
widespread appreciation of learned plagiarism or sensitive assimila-
tion, we can at least help to make great English poetry intelligible
by exposing the subject-matter of the classics, it becomes obvious
at once that Ovid is the classical author to start with. In the first
place, by treating his poetry as primarily a storehouse of great
fables, we are doing no more than everyone in Europe did for

D

centuries; one finds, for instance, that Jacques Legrand in
L'Archiloge Sophie (1405) defines *une poetrie* as a compendium of
stories to be used by poets either as themes or by way of illustration, and that it has two parts, the first consisting of stories from
the *Metamorphoses*, the second of stories from the Bible (v. Patter-
son, *French Poetic Theory*, Part I, Michigan, 1935). Whether it is
still possible for a work of literature to use Biblical themes, and
assume a knowledge of its stories, seems problematical; but it is
certainly true that, as Ezra Pound said years ago, '"we" have forgotten our Ovid, "we" being the reading public, the readers of
English poetry, have forgotten our Ovid since Golding went out
of print'.

The reference to Golding is apposite, for it is clear that the great
translations, which in their day brought to thousands of readers
some acquaintance with 'heathen mythology', should be made
to do duty again. At the same time a simple reprinting of Golding,
Sandys, Marlowe, and Dryden will not meet the case, for it is misleading to read a long poem (or any poem) in the dress of any one
period; even Keats seems to have thought of Homer as a kind of
magnified Elizabethan on the strength of Chapman — the music
reached him loud, but not clear, through Chapman's home-made
amplifier. A patchwork is better, for it shows up the absurdity of
any theory about the 'right' method of translation, besides fur-
nishing a practical illustration of the many kinds of music that
English has, in its time, played upon a single instrument.

The idea of a composite translation is not, of course, a new one;
Dryden supervised a version of the *Heroides* 'translated by divers
Hands, that you may at least have that Variety in the *English*,
which the Subject denied to the Author of the *Latin*', while something of the same kind was done for Homer in the *Oxford Book of
Greek Verse in Translation*, and for Baudelaire in a volume that
appeared about a dozen years ago. And for many reasons I think
it is a pity that someone does not do a similar job on Ovid. Such a
book would fill a good many gaps. The latinist who knows his

Ovid would find there a selection of the ways in which he has been englished; the unclassical would find a handbook to mythology, and much besides; and the student would not overlook the implicit commentary on the history of English poetry.

I say 'implicit', and, apart from the few generalizations that follow, have no intention of trying to make it explicit. It cannot really be done. What has been the influence of Ovid on English literature? What, for that matter, has been the influence of whisky on English politics? Such things are not, finally, subject to measurement. It is true that the siftings of scholars have provided us with material on the basis of which we may draw up certain quasi-numerical lists; but what to put into these lists, and how to use them when we have drawn them up, are questions which everyone would like someone else to answer. We may ascertain, for instance, that one poet has left in his work three hundred direct traces of Ovidian influence, while another has left thirty; but no one would care to say that it followed that the first poet was ten times as much under the sway of the inner spirit of Ovid's genius as the second. Shelley took the name 'Ianthe', obviously from Ovid, and gave it to the first child of his brain, the heroine of *Queen Mab*, and also to the first child of his body; what are we to say of this? Marlowe incorporated a phrase from the *Amores* in the last great speech of Dr. Faustus: down it goes in the list of references, but the passage in which it occurs could hardly be described as Ovidian. And when it comes to assessing the relative frequency of 'Ovidian' passages in English verse, all one can say is that they might crop up anywhere — even in our own day, as G. S. Fraser has shown in dealing with the poetry of Robert Graves.

Nevertheless, there is much interest, and some profit, in seeing how and when English poets have used the actual subject-matter of Ovid's work. The task of tracing these borrowings has long ago been carried out, of course, by the great army of commentators, and most of the knowledge available was summarized in 1912 by S. G. Owen in his indispensable essay, 'Ovid and Romance', in

G. S. Gordon's symposium *English Literature and the Classics* (Oxford). There the reader will find references to the dozens of major adaptations of Ovid in Chaucer and Spenser, Shakespeare's sonnets liv, lx, and cxxiii from the 'Pythagorean philosophy' of *Metamorphoses* xv, Jonson's *Poetaster*, with its concentration of the scattered autobiographical material, Chapman's *Ovid's Banquet of Sense*, incorporating echoes from *Amores* and *Tristia*, Heywood's four poems on the Golden, Silver, Iron, and Brazen Ages drawn from the opening of the *Metamorphoses* xiii as *The Contention of Ajax and Ulysses*, Aston Cokain's use of the *Tristia* and *Epistulae ex Ponto* in his *Tragedy of Ovid*. And the list, as its compiler well knew, could be extended over many more pages.

But surely there is more to it than that? What of the large and traceable part played by Ovid in the development of English prosody? The answer is that, admittedly, the elegiac couplet as written by Ovid acted as a stimulus to the growth of the closed 'heroic' couplet in English; poets well schooled in Ovid found that the nimbly antithetical style came one degree more easily to their pens. Pope, for instance, translated more than a quarter of the *Metamorphoses* at school; no doubt his translation was very much of an imitation, in method and manner, of Sandys's version, which he seems to have first read at the age of eight: so it becomes obvious that the achievement of such a man as Sandys, whom Dryden already built upon as 'the best versifier of the former age', helped the heroic couplet to reach the point of discipline at which Augustan poetry became possible. But this, after all, is only another manifestation of the great truth that each generation finds in literature what it goes to look for. In an earlier period Marlowe had found that his dogged and (for all its mistakes) literal rendering of Ovid's elegiac metre had led to a rough, emphatic couplet which foreshadowed the metre of Donne's *Satires*; does this mean that Donne, too, is to be reckoned among Ovid's poetic progeny? Metres are not formed solely by other metres; the rhythms of contemporary speech, the atmosphere of contemporary manners, the direction of contemporary thought, all play parts of equal importance. Virgil's hexameter produced Surrey's blank verse, but we do not call Shakespeare 'Virgilian' because *Hamlet* is written in blank verse; we reserve the adjective for certain passages in Tennyson and Milton which, though they too are in blank verse, and they too are derived from Virgil, bear no resemblance to Surrey's translation. Of course the technical influence was there, and Miss Wallerstein has described it for us very well; where Ovid gets an antithetical effect by the use of the caesura and then 'binds the two halves together by noun-adjective or noun-verb phrase or phrases suspended between the halves,' she writes, 'Sandys . . . substitutes the balance of separated half-line units with antithesis' (PMLA, 50, 1935). All the same, there is more to it than that. The fact that the late seventeenth century was able to find that kind of nourishment in Ovid was itself an effect, and not a cause. Influences, the small change of scholarly commerce, are in reality fairy gold, ready at a touch to turn to leaves.

THEORIES OF TRANSLATION

The history of the translator's attitude to his work, when pursued at length, is a surprisingly barren and irritating topic, in which a grain of true literary and historical interest lies buried beneath a mountain of theory and polemic. In spite of the length and urgency of the manifestoes with which they preface their work, translators are found on examination to be a docile race, easily led by the spirit of their times, and differing very little from their contemporaries. This gives a rather stifling atmosphere to their endless controversies, particularly as each generation has condemned the previous one without any serious study of its work. Restoration translators, for instance, generally assume that their Elizabethan and early seventeenth-century predecessors were all the slaves of a niggling literalism — an impression they could certainly not have gained from *reading* them. The historian's task here is not to accumulate material, but to trace the inner structure of the subject.

The real gist of the matter lies in the development, through the centuries, of a more and more sensitive literary conscience, and a more active historical imagination. Roughly speaking, one might say that the attention of the translator gradually shifts from the claims of the reader to the claims of the original, reaching an absurd climax in the early years of the present century, when the prevalent view was neatly hit off by Leslie Stephen:

> The modern translator is aware that Homer lived a long time ago and in a very different state of intellectual and social development, and he feels bound to reproduce the impression made upon the ancient Greek. The translator has to be an accurate scholar and to give the right shade of meaning for every phrase, while he has also to approximate to the metrical effect. The conclusion seems to be that the only language into which Homer could be adequately translated would be Greek, and that you must then use the words of the original. (*English Literature and Society in the Eighteenth Century*, 1904, cap. ii.)

If, then, translation is governed in its methods by a literary and historical conscience, it is obvious that we need not linger on the state of translation in the Middle Ages, for, to be short, it did not exist. The writer took his material, or claimed, for a variety of tortuous reasons, to have taken his material, from 'olde bokes' or a 'Frensshe booke', but you cannot have an attitude to translation unless you also have an attitude to plagiarism, and the Middle Ages had neither. Even so conscious an artist as Chaucer has evidently no clear-cut motive in referring to his sources. Sometimes it is a mere profession of faithfulness, as in *Troilus and Criseyde* I, 393 f.:

> And of his song naught only the sentence
> As writ myn auctour called Lollius,
> But pleinly, save our tonges difference,
> I dar wel seyn, in al that Troilus

> Seyde in his song, loo! every word right thus
> As I shal seyn.

At other times he refers his reader to the source as an excuse for
saving himself trouble, breaking off (for instance) an account of
the contents of Dido's letter to Aeneas with a weary

> But who wol al this lettre have in mynde
> Rede Ovyde, and in hym he shal it fynde.

The Elizabethans, here as elsewhere, give at first glance the
impression of carrying on mediaeval ideas quite unchanged. There
is still no sign of deference to the *manner* of the translated work;
the only new element is that the patriotic note gets stronger and
stronger. Whether the translator is dealing with a philosophic
work, a poem, or a treatise on ship-building, his claim is still the
same: the English mind needs the raw material of wisdom.

> As I therefore have to my small skill bestowed some labour about
> this peece of worke, even so could I wish with all my heart, profound
> learned men in the Greeke and Latin should make the like proofe,
> and every man store the tongue according to his knowledge and
> delight above other men, in some piece of learning, that wee alone
> of the world may not be still counted barbarous in our tongue, as in
> time out of mind we have bene in our maners. (Hoby, Preface to
> Castiglione's *Courtier*, 1561.)

As the sixteenth century draws to a close, stylistic questions
begin to assume more importance — for one thing, they provided
suitable weapons against rival translators — but there is no real
evidence that they actually govern anyone's practice. By listing
the arguments set out by the various translators in their prefaces,
it is possible to divide them into 'schools', to say that one prefers
a literal rendering, another favours free interpretation, and so
forth, but the body of their work tells a different story. The arguments back and forth, as summarized by Flora Ross Amos in her
Early Theories of Translation (Columbia U.P., 1920), leave one
dominant impression. In everything, Elizabethan and early Stuart

translators are practical men, seeking to increase the stock of wisdom, information, and entertainment available to their compatriots.

The claims of the original first make themselves heard, as one might expect, in the age of 'polite' letters which was dawning in the 1640's and attained its first splendour during the lifetime of Dryden. The word 'polite' has to carry inverted commas, since it would be absurd to say that, for instance, Milton's minor poems did not flower from the soil of polite letters in a very real sense: but the epoch in which literary matters were part of the equipment of the glass of fashion and the mould of form, ushered in by such figures as Waller, naturally had an immediate and profound effect on translation: middlemen have to be sensitive to the ups and downs of the market, more so than producers themselves.

Moreover, it was during the later seventeenth century that literary discussion was enriched by an idea which was, before long, to change its whole course; the idea, namely, of historicity. The concept of an intellectual climate varying from age to age, and from country to country, unknown in the Middle Ages, had developed slowly with the Elizabethans, whose idea of literary history was simply of a slow and narrow advance in which successive poets 'purified' the language and established useful precedents in the formal art of rhetoric. But during the lifetime of Dryden a flood of new conceptions swept away the narrow barriers of Renaissance literary judgement, and greatly increased the number of factors that were held to be capable of causing one work of literature to differ from another — climate, national genius, the 'spirit of the age'. These ideas, while not seriously affecting the practical business of translating, seeped into its theory, as can be shown by a comparison of, say, the pronouncements of Chapman with the Earl of Roscommon's *Essay on Translated Verse*.

Accordingly, it was after the Restoration that the loud and long debates began: what is the best metre? the best diction? the best critical programme? As the age became more scientific and more sophisticated, Method came into its own. The first thing to be established was, of course, the doctrine of suavity in language: formulated, with bland finality, by Hobbes.

> Another Vertue of an Heroique Poem is the Perspicuity and the Facility of Construction, and consisteth in a natural contexture of the words, so as not to discover the labour but the natural ability of the Poet; and this is usually called a good Style. For the order of words, when placed as they ought to be, carries a light before it, whereby a man may foresee the length of his period, as a torch in the night shews a man the stops and unevenness in his way. But when plac'd unnaturally, the Reader will often find unexpected checks, and be forced to go back and hunt for the sense, and suffer such unease, as in a Coach a man unexpectedly finds in passing over a furrow. (To The READER, concerning the VERTUES of an HEROIQUE POEM, prefixed to HOMER's ODYSSES, 1675.)

Again the controversy is mainly on side-issues; no one would seriously have quarrelled with the metaphor of a coach-ride, and argument was restricted to the size of the wheels and the kind of horse. A general basis of agreement is visible here as plainly as in the case of the Elizabethans. These translators see themselves as helping in the production of an English literature which will equal, and correspond with, the Greek and Roman: especially the Roman. Where their grandfathers had sought to increase the stock, they set themselves to make a contribution to polite letters, their aim being what we have now learnt to call 'cultural'. This was fostered by the habit of mind prevalent in the Augustan age, which was based on the deeply cherished conviction that England was the heir of Rome. What Rome had been to the ancient world, England would be to the modern. The eighteenth century, from Pope to Gibbon, is not properly intelligible until this has been grasped. One of its by-products was the great popularity of the genre known as 'Imitation', which was half translation and half a pleasant exercise in bringing the classics up to date by the sub-stitution of contemporary names. '"Imitations",' says Professor

Butt, 'are to be found amongst the poems of Congreve, Dennis, Diaper, Duke, Fenton, Hughes, King, Prior, Rowe, Stepney, Swift, Tickell, Walsh, Ward, and Wood', and if it were not for the fear of interrupting the neatly alphabetical order in which the names are arranged, it would be pleasant to add others, for, as Professor Butt says, 'This list does not pretend to be complete'. In their more patriotic moods, the Augustans even tend to give the impression that the classical authors, who after all were mere foreigners, should feel honoured at being taken up in this way. Dryden was not averse to taking this line when he wanted to flatter the Earl of Roscommon, and through him the Earl of Mulgrave, who had translated some Ovid:

> How will sweet *Ovid's* Ghost be pleas'd to hear
> His Fame augmented by a Brittish Peer,
> How he embellishes his *Helen's* loves,
> Outdoes his softness, and his sense improves?

Certainly it would hardly be fitting for a real, genuine peer to leave Ovid's work no better than he found it.

The position was slightly complicated by the fact that whereas Latin had two dominant metres, the elegiac couplet and the hexameter, English had only the couplet, so that the *Ars Amatoria* and the *Aeneid* both sounded rather alike when translated; but the self-confidence of the age was not ruffled by this. For those who hankered after metrical daring there was always the floundering and banal measure which was named, flatteringly, 'Pindarique', and which, in spite of Congreve's protest, remained a favourite metre, especially for translating from Horace, throughout this period.

And so, from about 1660 till the eighteenth century was almost spent, translators were substantially in agreement, wonderfully self-confident, and placidly convinced of the importance of their art. Dryden, with his genius for setting out the main facts of a case and drawing rapid and convincing deductions from them, had outlined the position to which Augustan translators were, in the main, to adhere, in his Preface to Ovid's Epistles (1680). There, we read of the three possible methods of translation: metaphrase, 'or turning an author word by word, and line by line, from one language into another', paraphrase, 'where the author is kept in view by his translator, so as never to be lost, but his words are not so strictly followed as his sense', and imitation, 'where the translator (if now he has not lost that name) assumes the liberty, not only to vary from the words and sense, but to forsake them both if he sees occasion'.

So affairs stood during the eighteenth century; and when the Romantics appeared, nothing very decisive was done (for the Romantic innovations were not, at any rate at first, *technical*). Admittedly, there had been a general feeling towards the end of the century that Homer ought to be translated into something that did not suggest Pope, and Cowper obligingly produced a version that limped somewhere in the wake of *Paradise Lost*: but the chief change of direction during the years 1780–1830 was in the choice of works to be translated. The classics were, on the whole, left to dons and clergymen, while brighter spirits translated from the modern languages. The days were over when the translation of classical literature was felt to be of such importance that the two great poets of their age, Dryden and Pope, could produce a body of translation which far outweighed their original work in bulk, and lagged not far behind it in popularity; when a large-scale translation of a large-scale classical author was an event of supreme importance; when Johnson could describe Pope's version of the *Iliad* as 'a performance which no age or nation can pretend to equal'.

A good example of the more liberal, and woollier, theorizing about translation that accompanied the deliquescence of the neo-classic mind, is furnished by *An Essay on the Principles of Translation* (1791) by Alexander Fraser Tytler, Lord Woodhouselee. Here, it is to be feared, the theory of translation has begun to slip into the morass of well-bred muddle in which it has lain ever since. Tytler's preliminary definition of a good translation swarms with ambiguities and evasions: it is, we read, 'that, in which the merit of the original work is so completely transfused into another language, as to be as distinctly apprehended, and as strongly felt, by a native of the country to which that language belongs, as it is by those who speak the language of the original work'.

On the surface, this is harmless, and gives a pleasant impression of fairness; but the word *merit* pulls the critical reader up. What of its faults? Are they to be omitted? If so, who is to decide what the faults are? Just how far Tytler's taste can be trusted may be seen from his contemptuous rejection of Milton's beautiful translation of Horace, Odes I, v: evidently he is not the man to do any important job of discrimination. And the implied refusal to consider any of the problems of literary history is borne out by the present tense of *is* and *speak*: Tytler is evidently thinking only of contemporary or recent literature. Yet, in fact, the body of the essay shows that he is equally willing to apply his doctrine to work of any age or nation; in Chapter III he singles out for approval Pope's treatment of the parting scene between Hector and Andromache (*Iliad*, vi, 466). Pope has left out the fact that the boy's nurse has a waist 'elegantly girt': Homer, says Tytler, 'has, in my opinion, shewn less good taste in this instance than his translator, who has, I think with much propriety, left out the compliment to the nurse's waist altogether'. In short, Tytler, although he imagines himself to be free from the narrowness of the Augustans (and has in fact abandoned their close-knit and consistent intellectual structure), is at one with them in adopting a cavalier attitude towards the original, favouring 'improvement' either by omission or addition. We are, accordingly, the less surprised when we find him repeating the Augustan condemnation of earlier translators on the grounds of their supposed literalism.

It was no doubt in reaction against this kind of *laissez-faire* blandness that the Victorian literary conscience, impressed by the ever-increasing volume of classical scholarship, made the theory of translation into a nightmare of bye-laws, with 'Trespassers Will Be Prosecuted' nailed to every tree-trunk. Arnold in his *On Translating Homer* (1861) made an effort to cut through the tangle by basing his argument entirely on the need for faithfulness to the four outstanding qualities of Homer, rapidity, directness of language, directness of ideas, and nobility. From the fundamental question, whether the translator can produce a work that will affect the modern reader in the same way that the original affected its audience, he sheers away by declaring that we have no means of knowing how the original audience was affected.

Once again the debate is largely on the surface, and translation is floating on the deep current of the age. This is not to say that the argument between Arnold and Francis W. Newman lacks interest (was it the crushing finality of Newman's retort, that load of bricks from beneath which Arnold emerged, still graceful, but bruised, that led to the poet's decision not to proceed with his own version of Homer?), but it is evident that both are specifically nineteenth-century, and yoked together so that the differences between them are slight compared with the gulf that separates either from earlier translators. For the broad notion underlying Augustan theories — that there is only one kind of poetry, and the best translation is that which, without too much monkeying with the original poem, reproduces it in this kind of poetry — has disappeared. The rise of a more powerful literary scholarship, and a broader, if less exact, taste, has done its work. And in any case the problem has lost much of its urgency. There was no longer an urgent demand for translations of the classics (except, no doubt, among schoolboys; but cribs are plain sailing); and the greatest translator of the age, Fitzgerald, was working from a language that no one else understood, and was therefore a law unto himself.

Since then there has been something of a renascence of translation, at any rate as far as poetry is concerned; the general idea seems to be that both the modern reader and the original text should be prepared to waive their claims to some extent, and submit to an even stronger claim, that of Poetry itself. The restrictive over-anxious Victorian theory killed the idea that it was any use trying to render a foreign poem 'exactly', and the ambition became that of trying to produce a good poem on the basis of the translated one, not too different in tone if possible: thus Mr. Eliot hailed Ezra Pound as 'the inventor of Chinese poetry for our time'. If this sounds like a reversion to the neo-classic idea of 'imitation', we should remember that the words 'inventor' and 'for our time' stress the relative nature of literary taste in a way quite alien to the idea of an historical cycle throwing up similar conditions. However much the original matters, it is clear that the translator is still inventing, in a sense, for all he is worth — he must at any time be ready to create a new kind of English poem to meet a special demand — and that he is labouring, in Rossetti's words, 'to endow a fresh nation, as far as possible, with one more possession of beauty'.

Along with the ebb and flow of theories — for theory, in literature, is always an attempt to rationalize and buttress the taste of the day — goes a corresponding rise and fall in the reputations of the various translators. The great recrudescence of interest in Elizabethan literature, fathered chiefly by Lamb's *Specimens* in 1808, brought Golding and Chapman back into favour, and with them, Sandys. Coleridge regretted that Chapman had not translated the *Iliad*, as well as the *Odyssey*, into decasyllabic couplets, as 'it might have saved us from Pope'. As the prestige of Elizabethan literature mounted, 'Tudor Translations' became increasingly fashionable. The series so named was begun in 1892 under the editorship of W. E. Henley, who published forty-four volumes; in 1925, Charles Whibley took over the general editorship and issued another fourteen. There were a few spirited protests: in 1911 Edmund Gosse was moved to declare, 'It may safely be asserted that viler trash, less representative of the original, less intelligent in intention, is not to be found in the literature of the world than in the feeble, vague and silly verse translations of the classics which deformed the earlier years of Elizabeth's reign'. But the tide of popularity swept the Elizabethan translators to such a pinnacle that no one, it seems, was moved to any adverse comment by Charles Whibley's wild overpraise of them in the *Cambridge History of English Literature*. So little was Whibley concerned with accurate assessment that he could even say of Golding's *Ovid*, 'You may read his mellifluous lines with something of the same simple pleasure that the original gives you' (C.H.E.L., IV, p. 20 — a gem pointed out to me by Mr. C. S. Lewis), thereby innocently bracketing one of the most sophisticated poets on record with one of the most utterly *naïf*. Compared with this, Ezra Pound's 'Can we, for our part, know our Ovid until we find him in Golding?' is the soul of moderation: at least it points towards a critical position, it is not mere gush.

ALLEGORY

Having taken this canter round the field, we must get back to Ovid. And when we begin to inquire into the reasons for his tremendous and enduring European fame, we see at once that one point overshadows all the rest in importance. It is that his reputation was firmly linked, throughout half a dozen centuries, with the allegorical method of interpretation. I say 'method', but of course allegory was never a mere method, elaborate as its technique became; it was, as everyone knows who has even scratched the surface of mediaeval thought, a way of thinking and, ultimately, of living. When that way of thinking died, it was not long before Ovid died too: that is, before the popular Ovid, eagerly studied and copiously quoted, gave way to the shorn and shunned figure, not fit to stand on the same shelf with Virgil, the Ovid of nineteenth-century literary taste. So much hinges on this question of allegory, with its consequent respect for the encyclopaedic, that a few of the chief facts must be passed in review.

'A few of the chief facts.' But even that is too large a claim. It would be nothing short of absurd for any but the most devoted specialist to attempt a sketch of the history of allegorical exegesis; so vast is the literature involved, so deep are the philosophic and historical issues which must be faced, that even with the aid of the many learned and subtle works in which modern scholars have illuminated corners of the subject, anyone who wishes to understand the allegorical tradition of European letters must pay it the compliment of a lifetime of study. For, if we start from the standpoint of our own age, how little we can know, to begin with, about the way in which the great myths have been understood: where did these myths originate? How were they regarded by the Greek and Roman poets by whose works we are chiefly introduced to them? What was Ovid's attitude to his Jupiter, his Iris, his Diana (not to mention his Philyra, Cerambus, or Lycaon)? Next, which of the many streams that flowed into the great river of allegorical exposition may be said to have influenced its course, and in what directions? Platonism, astrology, alchemy, the doctrines of the Fathers, all must be searched if we are to draw even an outline map of the subject. Even those questions arising from it which seem on the surface to be relatively simple prove, on inspection, to be of such complexity that very few authorities would care to attempt a definite answer. What, for instance, were the chief ways in which Christianity influenced the European attitude towards the profane myths? The Fathers denounced the myths as travesties of sacred history; there are evident links between this attitude and the attempt to justify the study of classical literature by claiming that the poets' fables conceal a deeper wisdom than the explicit statements of the philosophers. But was this concealment intentional, or were the poets building better than they knew? This question in its turn has an immediate bearing on another, an issue which for centuries exercised men's minds: what had become of the 'good pagans', those who, though worthy on moral grounds of reward in Heaven, had died before the advent of Christ, and therefore without baptism? If allegorical explanation could justify the study of their works, was it not possible for some extension of the same line of argument to maintain that their souls were also safe? It needs no special study of mediaeval and Renaissance thought to be aware of these and similar problems, for they erupt over and again into the best-known pages of English literature — in the long debate in *Piers Plowman*, for instance, or in Milton's identification of the fallen angels with the misleading and beautiful figures of pagan mythology which he himself, with so great a pang, rejected in his poetry, driving them forth into exile in the Nativity Ode, and rebuking them through the mouth of Christ in *Paradise Regained*. There are deep waters here, and I have no intention of drowning in them merely to give these notes a false air of completeness. Let it be enough for us that historians of the allegorical mode find its origins already too far back in Greek thought to be clearly defined, while the application of this method in the Christian tradition was firmly inaugurated by St. Paul (in, for example, the interpretation of Genesis xxi which he gives in Galatians iv, 22–31), though it was first fully systematized in Origen's commentary on the *Song of Songs*. From then on the way is fairly pointed, via the position adopted by Aquinas in the *Summa Theologica*, to Dante's famous words in the *Convivio*:

'— it should be known that writings can be understood and ought to be expounded chiefly in four senses. The first is called literal, and this is that sense which does not go beyond the strict limits of the letter; the second is called allegorical, and this is disguised under the cloak of such stories, and is a truth hidden under a beautiful fiction'. (Here follows an example from Ovid: Orpheus represents the power of wisdom) . . . 'The third sense is called moral; and this sense is that for which teachers ought as they go through writings intently to watch for their own profit and that of their hearers. . . . The fourth sense is called anagogic, that is, above the senses; and this occurs when a writing is spiritually expounded, which even in the literal sense by the things signified likewise gives intimation of higher matters belonging to the eternal glory'. (*Convivio* II, trans. Jackson, Oxford, 1909.)

E

The extent to which some mediaeval allegorizing was *voulu* is another thing that is too misty to be made out clearly. Some scholars have openly regarded the systematic exegesis of this or that poet as an attempt to give respectability to a literary preference already too strong to be ignored. Lester K. Born, in his invaluable 'Ovid and Allegory' (*Speculum* 9, 1934), pictures the Church, faced with the *fait accompli* of Ovid's popularity, working the thing out as a conscious strategy: 'What was simpler than to model the campaign upon that which had been so successful in the case of Vergil?' Certainly allegorization played the same part in the diffusion of polite letters as Bowdlerization today, though there are strong grounds for preferring the mediaeval nun's allegorized Ovid, as an educational instrument, to the modern high-school Shakespeare. Not being primarily concerned with the mediaeval mind, we can allow the matter to rest, with Professor Schevill's conclusion: 'Whether this method of finding hidden meanings was always sincere or not, is not evident in every case, and is unimportant to the study of the Renascence, but it made opposition to Ovid's growing popularity more and more ineffective.' (*Ovid and the Renaissance in Spain*, Berkeley, California, 1913.)

At all events, the gist of the story, as regards Ovid, is clear enough. The allegorization (and therefore, inevitably, the Christianization) of his work evidently begins about the time of Charlemagne, one of the leading originators of the process being Bishop Theodolfus, a poet and scholar of Charles's Court. This seems rather oddly late for the transformation to begin, Virgil, as Comparetti's great work made clear, having been allegorized some two centuries earlier; nevertheless, once begun, the work was carried on with enthusiasm. It culminated in two works of enormous influence, which spread the Christian interpretation of the *Metamorphoses* far and wide. These were the *Ovide Moralisé*, a vast French translation, dating from the early fourteenth century, which moralizes as it goes along, and the hardly less influential commentary composed at about the same time by Petrus Berchorius. The authorship of both these works has been the subject of dispute: the French writer has been identified, temptingly, with Chrétien de Troyes, while the work of Berchorius was long attributed to an English Benedictine, 'Thomas Waleys'. But the importance of each in the story of Ovid's conquest of Western Europe has never been in doubt. The *Ovide Moralisé* helped to carry the *Metamorphoses* wherever piety and learning could take it. Berchorius's commentary had to wait longer before its influence was felt, but it was printed at Paris and Lyons in the first decade of the sixteenth century, and was instrumental in handing on the mediaeval tradition of Ovidian allegory to the Renaissance, mingling therein with the handbooks of allegorized myth such as Boccaccio's *De Genealogiis Deorum*.

Having already abandoned the attempt to show clear lines of development, or even clear lines of argument, in Renaissance theories of allegory, we can merely note that the English translators of Ovid are conventional enough in their willingness to justify the study of their author on moral and even scientific grounds: the long-familiar arguments are served up in a more or less mechanical way. All that is necessary is to distinguish between strictly theological interpretation on the one hand, and more or less random moralizing and book-making on the other. While the second type can be found persisting right up to the very frontiers of the Augustan age, the first is more and more strictly curtailed after the beginning of the sixteenth century. It was, after all, only the first book of the *Metamorphoses*, describing the creation and early history of the world, that bore an obvious resemblance to the Scriptures (the building of the Tower of Babel corresponds to the revolt of the Titans, Noah and his wife appear as Deucalion and Pyrrha, etc.). Thus we find Arthur Golding, the chief Elizabethan translator of the poem, waxing theological enough in the first book, but confining himself to moral comment in the remaining fourteen. Yet in his apologetics Golding can be seen carrying on the mediaeval tradition boldly. In his prefatory Epistle, he asserts that the wisdom of the ancients agrees in substance with the truth of Scripture, and repeats the mediaeval opinion that the pagan poets were in fact familiar with the Old Testament ('What man is he but would suppose the author of this booke The first foundation of his woorke from Moyses wrightings tooke?'), and purposely wrapped the knowledge which they found there in allegorical form; after a survey of the 'evidence' he concludes:

> I trust there is alreadie shewd sufficient too detect
> That Poets tooke the ground of all their cheefest fables out
> Of scripture: which they shadowing with their gloses went about
> Too turne the truth too toyes and lyes . . .
> If Poets then with leesings and with fables shadowed so
> The certeine truth, what letteth us too plucke those visers fro
> Their doings, and too bring ageine the darkened truth too lyght,
> That all men may behold thereof the cleerenesse shining bryght?

In any case, sixteenth-century poetry, at least up to 1590, was for the most part heavily didactic and allegorical, employing its yokel diction and clumping metres in telling stories and adding long-drawn-out moralizations. (Spenser is — largely — an exception as regards the quality of his work, but entirely typical in his view that a poem's substance were best 'clowdily enwrapped in allegorical Devises'.) Examples of this homespun brand of allegorizing are numerous; Professor Douglas Bush, for example, has drawn attention (in *Modern Philology*, XXV, i, 1927) to one poem, occupying thirty pages in the collection *A Poore knight his Pallace of private pleasures* (1579), which uses the convention of the allegorical dream 'to describe a battle between the forces of Diana and Cupid and a trial before the gods'; he compares it, significantly, with the work of Lydgate. Among the Ovidian translators of the period, it is perhaps sufficient to mention Thomas Peend, whose version of *The Pleasant Fable of Hermaphroditus and Salmacis — with a morall in English Verse* appeared in 1565. Peend's 'fable' is given in 165 verses, his 'morall' in fifty-five. Few will ask for more than a brief specimen of his moral deduction:

> So we our cheefe and greatest Good,
>   the treasure of our minde,
> Do lose, and so to slauysh luste,
>   our nature free we bynd.
> And seruauntes bond vnto our wyll,
>   we warke our wretched woe.
> So one may lose hym selfe, and be
>   vnto hym selfe a foe.
> So do we chaunge the happy hope
>   of everlastyng ioye,
> Euen for the present pastyme, whych
>   our selves doth most anoye.
> We chaunge our nature cleane,
>   being made effemynat,
> When we do yeeld to serue our lust,
>   we lose our former state.

Even this does not exhaust Peend's determination to hang as much as possible of his mental wardrobe on to the Ovidian peg: we are next invited to discuss 'a pleasant Question', which turns out to be, how could Venus love Vulcan? For, as he takes eight pages to drive home, beauty is the usual incitement to love.

This has taken us some distance from our main thread — the continuance of the allegorical tradition in the study of literature from mediaeval into modern times — but not, I think, so far as to lose it. The point is that the allegorical habit was partly an austere and strictly applied method, and partly an excuse for anyone to read any useful moral lesson into any story; and the first usually slid into the second. The more sensible translators of Ovid have less of a gulf between theory and practice: Sandys, for instance — than whom no more sensible man has contributed to English literature — is sparing, in his great commentary, of random moral reflections, and equally sparing in his preface of extravagant claims for the wisdom of the ancients. His standpoint is very close to that of Bacon in the *Advancement of Learning*.

'The use of this feigned history hath been to give some shadow of satisfaction to the mind of man in those points wherein the nature of things doth deny it, the world being in proportion inferior to the soul; by reason whereof there is, agreeable to the spirit of man, a more ample greatness, a more exact goodness, and a more absolute variety, than can be found in the nature of things'. (*Advancement*, Bk. II, iii, 2.)

'For the Poet not onely renders things as they are; but what are not, as if they were, or rather as they should be, agreeable to the high affections of the Soule, and more conducing to magnanimitie: juster than either men or Fortune, in the exalting of Vertue and suppressing of Vice, by shewing the beauty of the one and deformitie of the other, pursued by the divine Vengeance, by inbred terors, and infernall torments'. (Sandys, *To the Reader*, ed. 1632.)

Nevertheless Sandys is far from wishing to throw overboard the mediaeval tradition of purely allegorical interpretation, and it is his avowed intention to bring the pagan stories, wherever he can, into line with the Scriptures, for the early history of the world is 'most obscurely and perplexedly delivered by all, but the supernaturally inspired Moses'. So, towards the middle of the seventeenth century, the pagan poets are held to be at any rate working on the same subject-matter as that of the Old Testament, even if they are not actually drawing their material from its pages.

So widely known a book must have been influential; as an illustration of this I suggest that we take a fairly close look at the explanation of his method offered by John Jones, the translator of *Ibis*, in 1658:

I may boldly say, there are not so many histories of [*sic*, for in] so few verses of any Poet now extant whatsoever. All these histories I have one by one, briefly and fully illustrated and explained, by collecting and comparing the several conjectives of the choicest Authors that have walked in that path. The most that I have stollen in composing this small piece of Illustration, was many hours snatch'd from night, and my own repose: For the day was not mine, but dedicated to that *Sisyphon*-toil of the Education of Youth. And to add, as it were a Mind to the Body, for the benefit of old and

young, I have brought home each history to our own selves by
Application. First Physical; for under the shadowing names of
fictitious Heathen Deities is covered the Body and Substance of
Natural Philosophy; Poets under Allegories expressing the wonder-
ful works of Nature. Secondly, Ethicall; For the utmost scope the
Poets aimed at, was not Fables, but Morality. Here be Precepts that
will inform the Understanding, reform the Affection, and direct the
Will: here are noble examples, inflaming the mind with candid
emulation, leading, as it were by the hand, through the temple of
Vertue, to the temple of *Honour*. Here be more perfect Rules than
those of Men or Fortune, in the exalting of Vertue and suppression of
Vice; shewing the Beauty of the one and deformity of the other.
Thirdly, Theological: for let a skilful hand modestly draw aside the
curtain of Poetry, there will fairly appear the sovereign face of the
Queen of all Arts, Divinity.

For:

— without all question, as before Letters the Ancients expressed
their conceptions in Hieroglyphicks, so did the Poets their Divinity
under Fables and Parables. In Poetry you may discern an Unity and a
Trinity. One God under several attributes and effects; Three persons
all Brothers, *Jupiter*, *Neptune*, *Pluto*. Their Ensigns, a three-forked
Thunderbolt, a three-forked Mace, a three-headed Dog. Three
Graces, three Fates, three Furies. In poetry are described the Joyes of
Heaven charactred by the Elysian fields, the Torments of Hell
deciphred in the burning lake of *Phlegeton*, and the Tortures of
damned *Ixion* and the rest.

Jones is very thorough; he must have been an excellent Sisyphus
in the Grammar school, and his book would be a good text-book
in mythology for twelve-year-olds today. His method can be seen
from the following illustration. After each short extract, usually
one distich, he has 'historical' notes, each followed by the moral
application: the whole neatly numbered and typographically
arranged for clarity.

> Or whom *Antaeus* armes press'd out of breath,
> Or Lemnian wives did put to cruel death.

1. *Antaeus* compelled forreigners to wrastle with him, and so strangled them with his matchless strength.

(1) Thus the mighty oppress the weak, as the greater fish devour the less: the brasse pot with one touch will crack the earthen; let the Brittler then keep off, with a *Noli me tangere*. If the Frog swells at the Ox he will burst, so a Peasant medling with a Potentate.

2. The women of *Lemnos* for despising the sacrifice of Venus, were by the Goddess made so lothsome, that their husbands left them, and lived with new wives abroad; at last coming home, the old slew the new wives and their husbands, with all the male-children, save one.

(1) If no relation, no Religion, no other motive can persuade, methinks women should serve and love God, that the God of love may not permit their husbands instead of love to lothe them.

These are more like notes, added to improve the occasion, than strictly exegetical work: Jones seems often not to care whether the point he brings out is 'in' the original or not, as the word 'methinks' indicates. I cannot resist giving another example: this kind of thing sends a ray of light straight into the heart of a past age.

> Or into Tartar from a rock fall dead,
> As he that *Platoes* book of death hath read.

Cleombrotus a Philosopher of the Academick sect, as soon as he had read the book called *Phædon*, concerning the immortality of the soul, compiled by *Plato*, who was scholar of *Socrates*, cast himself down from a rock into the sea, hastening to enjoy the happiness he had read of.

(1) *Summum nec metuas diem, nec optes*. Nor fear, nor wish thy latter end. Be not ashamed to live, nor afraid to die, nor hasten thy death in hope of a better life. The souldier ought not to move unless the commander give the word.

(2) Although our light afflictions are not to be compared to the eternal weight of glory immortal, though we have a crown of righteousness laid up for us, it is rather with patience to be expected, than preposterously to be snatched. The kingdome of heaven is not to be caught with such kind of violence.

(3) Those heathen Philosophers may rise up in judgment against these modern Hereticks, that do hold that the body and soul die together.

This shows the gulf between theory and practice: Jones is typical in that he brings in the full intellectual artillery of the allegorical method, in so far as it had survived into his day, and then feels himself free to improve the shining hour in any way that occurs to him. This is very Elizabethan; unless Jones was an old man, the spate of Tudor translations of piecemeal selections from the classics, accompanied by the appropriate moralizing, would be over some time before he was born, so it is an open question whether Jones, and people like him, were carrying on a tradition consciously or unconsciously.

At any rate, it should by now be firmly established that, until a mere two hundred years ago, Ovid, in common with all famous writers, was not merely enjoyed for his literary qualities, but studied as a source of wisdom. The story of how this view of literature changed, at first gradually, then with increasing swiftness, is the story of the end of a world; or rather part of that story, since the fate of allegory is only one effect of the earthquake which accompanied the transition from the mediaeval to the modern world. Just as Ovid's poetry came to be disliked on stylistic grounds — its essentially metropolitan, courtly, and self-conscious tone rang more and more hollow on the marble counter as the Victorian age approached, and the raw cult of sincerity took possession of the public taste — so the mythopoeic mind, which had created the *Metamorphoses* in the first place, and lovingly dwelt upon its fables for centuries, collapsed under the weight of empirical science. Not science alone, of course; for science never is alone: that is its strength. The study of pagan mythology had been attacked by the Puritans in the seventeenth century, while orthodox piety joined in the demand, voiced over and again in the criticism of the age of Dryden, for a Christian subject-matter in epic poetry. The objection to mythology on the ground that its fables are useless fiction was no novelty to Rymer, Cowley, le Bossu, or St. Evremond. The eighteenth century took over, with evident relish, the task of dissolving the tradition of respect for the myths, and their denunciations can be found in unexpected places. Thus Fielding, in his Interchapter on 'the marvellous' in *Tom Jones*, says that if it is impious to bring the Christian supernatural into fiction, it is 'horrid puerility to search the heathen mythology for any of those deities who have been long since deprived of their immortality'. This Gradgrindian outlook ('teach these boys and girls nothing but facts') remained something of a nuisance to imaginative writers until quite recently. Keats was evidently worried by it; that, at least, is how I interpret the sentence 'I hope I have not *in too late a day* touched the beautiful mythology of Greece, and dulled its brightness'. Since then, with the currency of a more sensitive distinction between truth and falsehood, the stock of the myths has risen again; especially since psychology, and in particular Jungian psychology, has been at hand to provide them with a free pass into any intellectual *milieu* whatsoever. But during the transition from one kind of respectability to another, from the shelter afforded by allegory to the shelter afforded by symbolism, there was certainly a feeling that the myths could never again be of much *use*. George Eliot, for instance, wants to show in Mr. Casaubon a picture of a brain-starved pedant, an intellectual remnant of the eighteenth century; so — a stroke of genius — she has him engaged on a great work to show 'that all the mythical systems or erratic mythical fragments in the world were corruptions of a tradition originally revealed'; such speculations, which to Golding and Sandys would have seemed laudable and even urgent, were mere futility as seen by a progressive Victorian. All this meant that the subject-matter of a poem like the *Metamorphoses* lost its importance. We must be careful, however, to confine this point to the pronouncements of critics and theorists. It was during this 'bleak' period, when the myths were sent wandering in the cold wind of rationalism, that English poetry produced its greatest mythological poems, from *Prometheus Unbound* to *Tithonus*. Poets, in short, have more *sense* than critics.

At any rate, Ovid, once the most securely anchored of the Latin poets, was blown out to sea when it was found that his moorings had rotted away. It is difficult, perhaps impossible, to pick out any decisive blast of this gale that could be said to have carried him further than the others, but I cannot help feeling that Addison's easy and contemptuous dismissal of the allegorical tradition must have carried great weight. He had translated some parts of the *Metamorphoses* for Garth's compilation (1717), and when reprinting them as part of his poetical works, he added a statement, 'Notes on some of the foregoing stories in Ovid's Metamorphoses', which is found in every subsequent edition. In this, as in all else, the method of 'Atticus' was to undermine the object of his attack rather than to push it over; and in this, as in all else, he was successful. When the suave voice begins to speak, the murmuring of the commentators is suddenly stilled, and their long labour is over.

> There are few books that have had worse commentators on them than Ovid's Metamorphoses. Those of the graver sort have been wholly taken up in the mythologies; and think they have appeared very judicious, if they have shown us out of an old author that Ovid is mistaken in a pedigree, or has turned such a person into a wolf that ought to have been made a tiger. Others have employed themselves on what never entered the poet's thoughts, in adapting a dull moral to every story, and making the persons of his poems to be only nick-names for such virtues or vices; particularly the pious commentator, Alexander Ross, has dived deeper into our author's design than any of the rest; for he discovers in him the greatest of mysteries of the Christian religion, and finds almost in every page some typical representation of the world, the flesh and the devil. . . . I shall therefore only consider Ovid under the character of a poet. . . .

Thus, quietly, the trick is done: centuries of allegorical exposition have become faintly ridiculous; a needless burrowing after 'what never entered the poet's thoughts'. In the face of this attitude, the tradition withered away very quickly. It is true that Pope, in his Preface to the *Iliad*, did not openly attack the idea that Homer had set out to 'clothe all the properties of elements, the qualifications of the mind, the virtues and vices, into forms and persons'; it would have been too much trouble, and in any case he gives the impression of not caring enough to enter into a possible controversy. And in any case, he says, it was only very early poets who had written with allegorical intent. 'For when the mode of learning changed in the following ages, and science was delivered in a plainer manner, it then became as reasonable in the more modern poets to lay it aside, as it was in Homer to make use of it'. The encyclopaedic tradition, a Siamese twin of the allegorical, could not hope to survive it for long; and although the great composite translation of the *Metamorphoses*, edited by Sir Samuel Garth in 1717, was actually reprinted in 1732 with an elaborate commentary on something like the old encyclopaedic lines, it was, significantly, the Abbé Banier who undertook that commentary. Banier was a powerful foe of the allegorical tradition, and author of a Euhemeristic survey of mythology which attracted sufficient attention to be englished in 1739 as THE MYTHOLOGY AND FABLES OF THE ANCIENTS, Explain'd from HISTORY. From this translation the English reader would learn that the study of myth was simply a waste of time unless it was regarded as a kind of poor relation of history.

> I own, for my part, if there was nothing in all the Fables of the Poets but some Allegories, I don't see what great value we ought to have for their Works: nothing to me would appear more insipid. Whereas, if it is true that they comprize ancient Facts, their making use of such numbers of Fables has nothing at all surprising; it gives us even a better opinion of the Genius of the *Greeks*, since we see that in spight of their invisible byas towards Fictions, they did not however feed themselves with Tales of mere Invention; and tho' they have embellished their Narratives, yet we know at least that they contain several Truths of Importance.

Banier's work marks an interesting stage in the historiography of myth; the age of the ponderous collection of facts is well under way (Frazer's edition of the *Fasti* can be seen approaching in the distance), while the theoretical basis of the study of myth is at its most cold, rationalistic, and thoroughly unadventurous. In his four volumes Banier reduces hundreds of myths to their presumed basis in historical fact, going as far afield as Egypt, and even touching on the 'Yncas of Peru', but, as was probably inevitable in an early eighteenth-century Frenchman, ignoring northern mythology altogether. His explanations range from plausible and sober reconstruction to dogged guessing on about the same level as the 'bloody:-by-Our-Lady' school of philology. He has, of course, an historical pigeon-hole ready for the allegorists themselves; at least he understood something of their governing ideas and assumptions, which is more than could be said of Addison: it was 'the *Platonick* philosophers', he says, who, to defend their religion from the onslaught of the Christians, 'pretended that these Fables were but Allegories, that wrap'd up grand Mysteries, and especially that of the different Productions of second Causes, animated by the same Spirit that had disintangled and extracted them from the Chaos where they were blended in confusion: That the Multiplicity of Gods, with worshipping whom they were reproach'd, were only Genii, of an inferior order to the first Mover, who had committed to them the Government of the World.' So Banier threw the powerful resources of his knowledge into supporting the view that myth was a disguised or distorted piece of history. This view was, of course, very appropriate to the age of Reason, and has since received a number of crushing blows as the study of myth has advanced; those who imagine, however, that Euhemerism has breathed its last, will find it instructive to read the articles on myth in the *Oxford Classical Dictionary*.

Only one comment remains to be added. Writers on the subject often assume, in a curiously simple-minded way, that allegory, as a habit of mind, is dead. As a formal approach to literature, of course, it is; but the habit of mind that seeks to expound a text by plunging a bucket into the well of its profundities and examining what comes up — that habit, as everyone knows who has sat, Sunday by Sunday, through the sermons at a provincial parish church, has never died or even sickened. Mr. Priestley, in his *English Journey*, found it among the Nonconformists of Birmingham:

> The sermon itself, which was not a bad one, had not changed much; there was the same trick in it of taking a tiny and apparently meaningless text — such as *Then Saul went up* or *These likewise cast lots* — and then finding an astonishing number of deeply significant meanings in it; a method that would soon turn any book, a *History of Rutlandshire* or *Commercial Guide to Sweden*, into a work of the profoundest wisdom.

The funny thing is, it *would*.

The Figure of the Poet

An attitude towards a poem, or an *œuvre*, implies (nearly always) an attitude towards the poet. The English view of Ovid's personality has developed rather interestingly, and merits some attention here. In beginning, for the sake of completeness, with the *aetas Ovidiana* — the name given by Ludvig Traube to the twelfth and thirteenth centuries in Europe — it is useless to try to crystallize out any particularly *English* view; this country was not, in such matters, an island until Tudor times.

Biography proper evolved slowly from the mediaeval introductions and commentaries which distributed information piecemeal under various headings. The mediaeval commentator saw his task as divided into various categories or 'questions': faced with a literary work, he wished to establish the causes of its origin, the material of which it was composed, its intention, the useful lessons to be learnt from it, its title, and the branch of philosophy to which it belonged (*materia, invenio, utilitas, titulus, philosophie suppositio*). Anything the commentator knew, or thought he knew, about the life of Ovid was put in as it appeared apposite in one section or another; thus information that was deemed relevant in an introduction to the *Tristia*, say, would be omitted in an introduction to the *Metamorphoses*. The first account of Ovid's life which makes an approach to completeness is that prefixed by the twelfth-century writer Arnulf of Orleans to the *Metamorphoses*: his reason for covering the whole of the poet's life was that he was dealing with his major work, and it is not until the fourteenth and fifteenth centuries that full lives appear in commentaries on the minor poems. The humanistic attitude towards the poet's life evolved thus slowly from the mediaeval *accemus*. (I am getting all this from Dr. F. Ghisalberti's 'Mediaeval Biographies of Ovid', *Journal of the Warburg and Courtauld Institutes*, Vol. IX, 1946.)

Biography, like everything else, was harnessed to allegory by the mediaeval mind. Even the significance of Ovid's names did not go unrecognized: he was 'Ovidius' because he had written of the elements that went to form the universe, of which the egg, with its four substances arranged concentrically, was the symbol. He was 'Naso' because he had a nose which could distinguish keenly between the different odours of vice and virtue. Was this interpretation still faintly alive in the mid-nineties of the sixteenth century when Holofernes said, 'Ovidius Naso was the man: and why, indeed, Naso, but for smelling out the odiferous flowers of fancy, the jerks of invention'?

Mediaeval commentators generally trace Ovid's banishment to amorous intrigue. In the fifth century, Sidonius Apollinaris had identified Corinna as 'Caesarea puella': most mediaeval biographers make her the wife of Augustus. The charges against Ovid are commonly said to be three: that he had committed adultery with the Empress, that he had involuntarily seen Augustus in some disgraceful circumstances, and that his works had a corrupting influence. The story of the poet's banishment was accompanied by a tradition, accepted by (among others) Boccaccio, that he was later repatriated, and suffocated to death among the crowds who flocked to welcome him to Rome.

The gift for finding on the written page exactly what one is looking for, did not desert the men of the Renaissance. The Elizabethan attitude towards Ovid was rich and complicated — some of its features we have already noted under the heading 'Allegory' — but there can be no doubt that one of its strongest elements was the conception of the poet as an aesthetic libertine. There was — and this is odd — no sixteenth-century English translation of the *Ars Amatoria*, but such works as Chapman's *Ovids Banquet of Sence*, Shakespeare's *Venus and Adonis*, and Marlowe's version of the *Amores* indicate, in their different ways, that the Elizabethans welcomed Ovid as the poet of anti-respectability: Marlowe's book, which included as an additional *divertissement* Sir John Davies's largely obscene epigrams, was evidently aimed at a *succès de scandale*, and all the copies the authorities could lay their hands on were in fact publicly burnt, by order of the Archbishop of Canterbury and the Bishop of London, on June 4, 1599.

This impression is supported by the very interesting chapter on Jonson's *Poetaster* in Mr. Oscar James Campbell's *Comicall Satyre and Shakespeare's Troilus and Cressida* (San Marino, California, 1938). His view is, briefly, that Jonson was attacking the vogue of sophisticated sexual corruption which was rampant among the young nobility of the 1590's, for whom the then 'fleshly school' of poets wrote. This 'philosophy', with Ovid's didactic love-poems as its inspiration, exalted the passions above reason, to this end perverting the arts of literature and living; and was moreover an unhealthy element in the life of the socially elect which was fatally easy for their inferiors to imitate — or, rather, to parody, since one of Jonson's favourite satiric themes is always the mis-guided and ridiculous attempt of cits and parasites to ape the fashions of the *élite*. Accordingly, we are shown three levels of social and intellectual conduct. The first is inhabited by Virgil and Horace, who recognize and defend the dignity and nobility of poetry, and the claims of virtue; the second by Ovid, Propertius, and Tibullus, who, in many ways admirable and sympathetic, are living in a world founded on a mixture of fantasy and self-indulgence; while the third stratum is composed of those (Chloe, Crispinus, Demetrius, Tucca, and the rest) who are trying vainly to break into the second. This leads to a very significant view of Ovid's character; while closer to an understanding of the true nature of poetry than his father and his father's hangers-on, he is further from it than Virgil, Horace, and Caesar himself. Caesar in fact is given a speech in which he reveals an attitude very close to what classical scholars tell us was the opinion of Augustus:

> Sweet *poesies* sacred garlands crowne your gentrie:
> Which is, of all the faculties on earth,
> The most abstract, and perfect; if shee bee
> True borne, and nurst with all the sciences.
> Shee can so mould *Rome*, and her monuments,
> Within the liquid marble of her lines,
> That they shall stand fresh, and miraculous,
> Even, when they mix with innovating dust;
> In her sweet streames shall our brave *Roman* spirits
> Chace, and swim after death, with their choise deeds
> Shining on their white shoulders; and therein
> Shall *Tyber*, and our famous rivers fall
> With such attraction, that th'ambitious line
> Of the round world shall to her center shrinke,
> To heare their musicke: And, for these high parts,
> CAESAR shall reverence the *Pierian* artes.   (V, i)

Compare this with Suetonius's account of the literary taste of the historical Augustus; who, he tells us

'— in his Greek and Latin reading sought for nothing so keenly as precepts and examples of salutary application to the commonwealth or to individuals. These he copied word for word; and, suiting the admonition to particular requirements, would frequently despatch to members of his household, to his captains and principal governors, or to magistrates at Rome'.

F

It seems clear that Ovid's banishment, coming as it does immediately after his most daring act of presumption (the poets and their friends have got up a masque at which they impersonate the deities of official religion, and Ovid, as Jupiter, has sent a messenger to 'command' Caesar to send Julia to the party), is seen by Jonson as a richly deserved punishment, and part of the general purge which in the next act extends to the hangers-on of the courtly set.

Though Mr. Campbell's view has met with authoritative opposition, I am bound to mention it here because it convinces me. The whole interplay of the characters bears it out. Chloe, the minx who has married a citizen 'because I heard indeed, they kept their wives as fine as ladies; and that wee might rule our husbands, like ladies; and doe what wee listed', is condescendingly flattered by the courtly set (Julia invites her to come to court, and Ovid himself says, 'I see, even in her lookes, gentrie, and generall worthinesse'), and takes part, along with her scabby followers, in the masque that brings the trouble to a head. The decree which Jupiter–Ovid issues at the beginning of the party is a pretty savage travesty of the doctrines of the real Ovid:

> The great God, IUPITER,
> Of his licentious goodnesse,
> Willing to make this feast, no fast
> From any manner of pleasure;
> Nor to bind any God or Goddesse,
> To be any thing the more god or goddess, for their names:
> He gives them all free licence,
> To speak no wiser, then persons of baser titles;
> And to be nothing better, then common men, or women;
> And therefore no God
> Shall need to keep himselfe more strictly to his Goddesse,
> Then any man do's to his wife.
> Nor any Goddesse
> Shall need to keepe her selfe more strictly to her God
> Then any woman do's to her husband.
> But, since it is no part of wisdome,

> In these daies, to come into bonds;
> It shall be lawfull for every lover,
> To breake loving oathes,
> To change their lovers, and make love to others,
> As the heate of every one's bloud,
> And the spirit of our *nectar* shall inspire.
> And IUPITER, save IUPITER.

Nor can there be any doubt that Caesar's wrathful descent, and his banishment of Ovid, are meant to be seen as the actions of a just ruler; he later magnanimously pardons Gallus and Tibullus, who were both among the masquers, with 'Resume into the late state of our love. . . . You both are gentlemen'; not the tone of a martinet or tyrant.

Jonson's stern warning seems to have had a very limited effect; at any rate, interest in the 'romantic' features of Ovid's personal history was now fully aroused, and the early seventeenth century saw a tendency among translators to exploit the pathos of his banishment in a sufficiently heavy-handed fashion. Wye Salton-stall, who issued translations of the *Heroides* and *Tristia* in rapid succession (1636 and 1637), had evidently decided that Ovid would make a hit with his feminine readers. By way of preface to the *Heroides* he provides two dedications, one in prose and one in verse, with identical headings: 'To the Vertuous Ladies and Gentlewomen of England'; whom he addresses in terms well calculated to widen Ovid's public.

> Your beauties (Ladies and Gentlewomen) are but types and shadowes of the beauty of your vertuous mind, which is discerned by Noble and Courteous actions. I may therefore presume that *Ovid*'s Heroicall Epistles, chiefly translated for your sakes, shall find a gentle acceptance, suitable to your Heroicall dispositions, for Curtesie and Ingenuity, are the companions of Gentility.

With his *Tristia* he continued the process of laying it on thick; an ornamented title-page shows the stages of the poet's life — fame, banishment, and death — while its significance is hammered home in couplet form by 'The Explanation of the Frontispiece' on the opposite page. Again, Saltonstall is willing to adopt whatever explanation of Ovid's banishment happens to suit his purpose: in his *Tristia* he informs the ladies that the poet's love for Julia was the cause of the catastrophe; in his *Heroides* the two other available explanations are given, when he makes Ovid say, in the prefatory '*Umbra Ovidii* or Ovids Ghost':

> By an error I great *Caesars* wrath did move,
> And then by writing of the Art of Love.

The reasons for the banishment continued to occupy the minds of Ovid's English biographers as long as the sentimental-romantic period of his fame lasted. 'The cause of his banishment is uncertayn,' wrote Thomas Underdowne in 1569, 'but most men thinke, and I am of that opinion also, that it was for using too familiarly Julia, Augustus his daughter, who of hir selfe too much enclined to lasciuiousness, was the more incensed therto by him, unto whom he wrote many wanton Elegies, under the name of Corinna.' If among 'most men' Underdowne wished to include serious scholars, he was in error; all the possible explanations are consistently kept in mind by the more moderate biographers: the cautious Sandys, in 1632, merely stated the alternatives, though he too testifies to the popularity of the more picturesque explanation ('Most agree that it was for his too much familiaritie with JULIA the daughter of AUGUSTUS, marked under the name of CORINNA'.) Sir Aston Cokain, whose undistinguished play on the subject was published in 1669, makes Ovid himself survey the evidence with commendable thoroughness, coming to the conclusion that the whole thing was a mistake.

Enter Ovid, *solus.*

> Sure I was born when all the glorious Stars
> Were met in Councel to contrive a Mischief.
> Under pretence of my Loose usefull studies,
> For the composing of my Art of Love,

In my declining years (when I expected
Ease, and a quiet life) I was exil'd
From *Rome*, and here confin'd to end my dayes
Among a people rude, and almost barbarous,
Except a few of th'Gentry and Nobility . . .

A many have imagin'd *Julia*
Daughter of great *Augustus*, was too gracious
And liberal of her Amorous Favours to me;
Which caus'd him to inflict this Punishment.
But ere that Emperor left the world, he was
Inform'd (for that Particular) of my Innocency:
And was acquainted that, if I were faulty,
It was an Error in me, not a Crime;
For if I ere enjoy'd her, it was through
Her craft; I taking her to be another.
But he was too severe; that excellent Princess
He shew'd as little Mercy to, as me.
Now about Twenty years, in the small Island
Of *Trimerus* (near the *Apulian* Shores)
Confin'd by him, sh'hath led a tedious Life.
I must confess she had a Generous kindness
For me, and took delight to read my Poems.
But by her Letters, and Authentick witness,
Clear'd me sufficiently from that Reproach:
And won thereby so much upon her Father,
That I had been repeal'd if he had liv'd.
Since his Decease by divers Messengers
(Persons of Noble Rank and Quality)
And by her eloquent Epistles she hath
(For my return to *Rome*) importun'd much
The great *Tiberius*, her too cruel Husband.
But he that to a Wife (who brought him all
The Universe in Portion) shews no mercy,
Will not redress my wrongs. Here I must mourn
Out all my life, and find my Funeral Urn.

                                                    Exit.

As always, life imitated literature, and Ovid's poetry can be seen
as an influence on conduct at the court of Charles II. Hamilton's

Memoirs of the Count of Grammont gives us an entertaining glimpse: 'the fair Jennings', having fallen out of love with Jermyn, and wishing to 'strain her resentment' 'still further', took a hint from the Dryden version of the *Heroides*:

> Ovid's *Epistles*, translated into English verse by the greatest wits at court, having lately been published, she wrote a letter from a shepherdess in despair, addressed to the perfidious Jermyn. She took the epistle of Ariadne to Theseus for her model. The beginning of this letter contained, word for word, the complaints and reproaches of that injured fair to the cruel man by whom she had been abandoned. All this was properly adapted to the present times and circumstances. It was her design to have closed this piece with a description of the toils, perils, and monsters, that awaited him in Guinea, for which he quitted a tender mistress, who was plunged into the abyss of misery, and was overwhelmed with grief and despair; but not having had time to finish it, nor to get that which she had written transcribed, in order to send it to him under a feigned name, she inconsiderately put this fragment written in her own hand, into her pocket, and, still more giddily, dropped it in the middle of the court. Those who took it up, knowing her writing, made several copies of it, which were circulated all over the town.

This was, indeed, the last age during which Ovid could be accepted as a teacher, for the life of pleasure was never thereafter to recapture that particular urbanity. If we compare the assumptions underlying the *Ars Amatoria* with those that govern Congreve's comedies, we see that the dramatist has all the Ovidian equipment in his scenes, including here and there a Dipsas; there is, of course, a tenderness latent in his view of love to remind us that Christianity and Chivalry had reached his bloodstream, if not his inkwell; but the Ovidian flavour is there, and it is not surprising that Congreve joined in a collective translation of the *Ars Amatoria* into Augustan couplets (1709). But it was a withering Ovid who lingered, rather unhappily, in the background of Restoration erotics. The days of his solid glory were numbered. Congreve himself was born too late, and retired from literature at the age of forty. As the eighteenth century advanced, English interest in Ovid, as a poet and as a human being, declined. The new literary taste was hostile to his artificiality, preferring high, if rather homespun, seriousness. Thomas Warton considered him 'at once rapid and abrupt. He wants dignity: he has too much conversation in his manner of telling a story'.

Ahead lay only the desert of Victorian facetiousness; as a horrible example let me quote from one John Jump's preface to his version of the *Heroides*, or, as he calls them,

> the charming Epistles of Ovidius Naso. Why should the Cantab and the Oxonian monopolize a delightful feast? Why not you, O general reader, be admitted to a table as invitingly served? Come in, good friend; the baked meats consist of a faithful rescript of the prettiest love-letters you ever perused, save certain correspondence perhaps between yourself and you know who.

That was in 1857. In 1957 it may well be that Ovid's reputation is mounting again, and that his poetry may once more be taken seriously. However that may be, his reign has been long, his influence vast, and his name powerful.

> Quaque patet domitis Romana potentia terris,
> Ore legar populi, perque omnia saecula fama,
> Si quid habent veri vatum praesagia, vivam.

> For, where-so-ere the *Roman* eagles spread
> Their conquering wings, I shall of all be read:
> And, if we Prophets truly can diuine,
> I, in my liuing Fame, shall euer shine.

(1949–56)

THE LIBERATION OF WORDSWORTH

In the world of ideas revolutions can happen unobtrusively, almost silently. In the field of English literature we are at the moment in the midst of an enormous revolution, almost a complete reorientation of taste. It is taking place rather in the manner of a change of season; not very obvious from one day to another, but impossible to overlook in its general effect. I mean the reassimilation of nineteenth-century poetry into the twentieth-century consciousness. Twenty years ago, when the inherited standards of 'romantic' literary taste were being pushed aside to make room for the newly discovered Metaphysicals and Augustans, all nineteenth-century poets, even the best of them, suffered a bad slump, while the good but not great poets of that epoch, such as Tennyson, fell into actual contempt. Now, the generally accepted view would be more or less what Mr. Graham Hough says at the end of his little handbook, *The Romantic Poets*:

> There was a few years ago a real danger that the Romantic age would come to be regarded, as the eighteenth century once was before it, as an unfortunate interregnum in our poetic history. [But] The Romantic movement does hold out a living hand to us, and not to grasp it is a kind of intellectual and emotional treason. We can perhaps see the results of the deliberate refusal of the romantic experience in this century in the present decay of creation, and the desiccation of much of our criticism . . . the difficult reabsorption of nineteenth-century values is one of the things that is needed for the mental health of the twentieth.

Most people, perhaps, would not make the issue quite so dramatic; I don't see that the twentieth century has suffered from 'a decay of creation' — its record in literature is surely a splendid one, and modern criticism (granted that there is at any time a fearful shortage of good criticism) seems to me very respectable. But, as I say, that is how people are beginning to see it. Slowly, rather painfully, and without any brouhaha or clique scheming, the major Romantics are swimming back into our ken.

But within this larger revolution there are several smaller, sharper ones that have to take place first before the wider issues can be settled, or even seen clearly. The two chief of these, to my mind, are the rescue of Wordsworth and the defence of Yeats. These two are, if not the greatest, at any rate as great as anyone in the world of romantic poetry; take Wordsworth away and the period would be without an effective beginning; take Yeats away and it would be without an effective end. Yet both these key figures have attracted some of the silliest criticism ever concocted. The reason is that they are both poets whose work was based on what could loosely be called a 'system'; in Wordsworth it is the Nature-mysticism; in Yeats it is the gyres, phases of the moon, arcons, and all the rest of the hocus-pocus. The result has been that one has to dig through twenty volumes of commentary on either poet before coming upon a paragraph of honest criticism of his poetry as poetry. I speak of the 'defence' of Yeats, because in his case the system-mongers have not quite strangled him yet; he is still read as a poet by people who conceive themselves to be enjoying a literary experience rather than studying occult philosophy. But all that is changing fast. Another half-dozen books of solemn comment on his idiocies, so solemn that it makes them more important than his poems, and he will be lost to us.

Already the subject is one on which people are alarmingly quick to misunderstand plain language. I once made a reference somewhere to 'the Gipsy Petulengro tradition of Yeats criticism', and this got itself quoted in a pamphlet on Yeats by G. S. Fraser; the pamphlet in its turn was reviewed by Miss Kathleen Raine, who was moved (by the quotation, obviously) to some rather superior comments about 'young critics who think Yeats was a kind of Gipsy Petulengro, and cannot understand how he wrote such great poetry when his general ideas were so silly' — words to that effect. I assure Miss Kathleen Raine that I do understand, very

well, how Yeats could combine being a great poet with having a
mystagogue's ideas on general subjects, and of course it was not
him but his critics I was comparing with Gipsy Petulengro: the
only point of bringing up so small a matter is that it shows how
hard it is to talk about the question at all without being immediately misunderstood.

If you want to know what is going to happen to Yeats, at this
rate, just look at what has happened to Wordsworth in the century
since his death. He has been cornered by the 'Wordsworthians' —
good, gentle souls who share, or think they share, his attitude
towards Nature and in consequence treat his writings as a Sacred
Book, on which it would be blasphemous to use the ordinary
methods of literary criticism. Turn over any of the great mound of
books the Wordsworthians have produced. Everywhere it is the
same story. Wordsworth as a religious teacher. — Was he Orthodox or Pantheist? — What happened to him on Snowdon? —
What is it *exactly* that dwells in the light of setting suns? — What
is the significance of his having to cling to a gate-post on the way
to school to convince himself of the reality of the external world,
or lie flat on the ground to bring the blood to his head before
seeing visions, or put his braces on outside his jacket to bring his
waistcoat closer to his diaphragm, or whatever the silly business
consisted of? They are admirably painstaking and devoted, these
books; several of them, indeed, such as those of Miss Helen
Darbishire and the late J. C. Smith, show all the acumen and
devotion which we expect from their celebrated authors. But
mark what was happening. While all this discussion was piling up,
this business of treating Wordsworth as if he were a cross between
Gandhi and Plato, the 'ordinary' reader of poetry was quietly
taking the hint to keep away. Without meaning to put anyone off
their idol, the Wordsworthians had done so, and very effectively.
They had done it by the simple means of setting up two different
kinds of approach to poetry; one that they used for Wordsworth,
and one that they used for all the other poets in the world.

To pick up one of these books and read it in the same evening as Mr. Bateson's[1] is an extraordinary experience. You would hardly guess that he and they were talking about the same subject. Mr. Bateson takes Wordsworth on his own terms, as a poet; he talks about the literary method of his work, as if that were important (which it is)! As if Wordsworth had ultimately to stand or fall on the merits of his poems, as created things, as artefacts (which he has)! It is a real rescue. Here is the new criticism of Wordsworth: I don't necessarily mean to say that Mr. Bateson is 'the *first* to sail Into the Arctic seas', because I think the thing has been going on, quietly, for some time, and people tell me that Mr. Jones's *The Egotistical Sublime*, which I have not yet read, has something of the same quality. What matters is that Wordsworth is being rescued; let us fervently hope that Yeats, with equal skill and bravery, will be defended.

However, as I am far from going along with Mr. Bateson's book all the way, I must now introduce a few discords into this fanfare of praise. To begin with, it seems possible that he has fallen into a separate but related error: that of substituting author-psychology for criticism. He says at the end of the first chapter that, as the poems are psychological documents, we have to approach them through a study of Wordsworth as a case-history:

> Since the poems are either the direct or the symbolic expression of his personal feelings, moods and intuitions their interpretation must depend upon a reconstruction of the evolution of the affective undercurrents of his personality. It will be necessary therefore to try and define states of mind of which Wordsworth was not wholly conscious himself, which he sometimes misunderstood or tried to suppress.

If this is true, it is of course tantamount to denying that Wordsworth was a great poet, or even, in a sense, a poet at all. Every poem, every work of art, is 'the direct or symbolic expression' of the man's 'personal feelings', but if we cannot come to a decision

[1] F. W. Bateson: *Wordsworth: A Re-Interpretation*. (Longmans.)

about its quality without going outside it, to the biography, that means that some very essential element, some vitamin, is missing from the work itself. It is always tempting, when one has enjoyed a poem, to root about among the biographical element for a few side-lights on it; but if this is erected into a system it becomes an admission that the work will not do as it stands. And, however cleverly and sympathetically it is done, we are back in the Public Library scene in Joyce's *Ulysses*, listening to the clevershins explaining that Shakespeare wrote a tragedy about Hamlet because he had just lost a baby son called Hamnet, and the similarity of the names is an important clue. It is a procedure more justified in Wordsworth's case than in almost any other, and we all do it, but that very fact is a damaging criticism of his work, and I cannot find that Mr. Bateson goes into the matter at all. Statements like 'The rhythm of his neurosis seems to have demanded at a certain stage in its sexennial progress a withdrawal from promiscuous social intercourse and a period of intense attachment, emotional and intellectual, to two or three intimates,' have the effect of making me wish, wildly, for a criticism of Wordsworth that would be absolutely impersonal and objective.

The trouble is (and I repeat that it is a mark *against* Wordsworth) that such a criticism, interesting and valuable as it would be, is hardly foreseeable. It would not be complete enough; Wordsworth was a psychological poet, and the mind he studied was the only one he had the opportunity (or, with his fearful egocentricity, the power) to study fully: his own. It is a question, rather, of distinguishing between the personal elements in his work which are relevant to a proper judgement and those which are not. The biographical, psychological facts which underlie the great split between 'early' and 'late' Wordsworth are, as I see it, relevant; the imaginative and mystical experiences of his childhood, about which so much fuss is commonly made, much less so. They are fully contained *within* the poems; furthermore, they are not peculiar to Wordsworth: every child has something of the sort; indeed, it is their universality that makes them an interesting subject for poetry.

But the question of the drying-up of Wordsworth's poetic powers is another matter. It has been much debated, like all Wordsworthian questions, in a curiously muddled and acrimonious way. (Coleridge, in the chapter of *Biographia Literaria* in which he 'answered' Wordsworth's arguments about the language of poetry, started this habit of going all round the pole to get to the next street, which has somehow clung to Wordsworth criticism ever since.) Thus there is to this day a good deal of rather undisciplined discussion as to whether it is, in the first place, true that Wordsworth 'went off' at all in his later years: both sides make exaggerated claims. Examined coolly, it is not really a very difficult question. Wordsworth wrote poetry over a period of sixty-five years, from 1785 to 1850; he himself said in the *Immortality Ode*, written in 1803, that something had gone wrong and his imagination didn't seem to be working as it had done when he was a child, and in the *Prelude*, which he was writing at about this time, he made a great point of the importance of a certain kind of imaginative or mystical experience that he used to have when he was younger but had not been familiar with since he grew up. And in fact it is true that the poetry he wrote after about 1807 is in some respects less original and arresting than the earlier work. It is still good, and in many places superb, but it is the work of a skilful, experienced, sensitive poet of the status of, say, Tennyson, rather than of a genius. And the earlier poems, flawed as they are, do read like the work of a genius. That is all; surely the disputants can calm down.

What gives the dispute its underlying acrimony, of course, is the personal rancour which so many have felt, and still feel, against the later Wordsworth, the man who became Controller of Stamps, held reactionary political views, wrote piously moral verses, and in general tried to live down the young poet who had preached Godwinian anarchism and fathered an illegitimate child in France. This reaction must already have been strong at the time when Browning's *The Lost Leader* was supposed (wrongly?) to refer to Wordsworth. I think these two strands need separating; obviously the old Wordsworth was not so much fun as the young one, but this has not much direct bearing on the quality of his work, because, as we saw in the case of Yeats, you can be very silly as a man and still admirable as a poet — unfortunately. I don't, as it happens, think that Wordsworth turned Tory and Pillar of Society in middle age just to be nasty: I think it was because he was unhappy and full of inadequacies and needed something to be certain about, like Dr. Johnson; it may even be true, as Mr. M. E. Burton maintained in his book, *One Words-worth*, that many of the alterations in the *Prelude* which look like attempts to make it more respectable were really motivated by a desire to make it a better poem. He just thought (wrongly, as it happens) that it read better that way.

None of this, as I say, is really to the point, though admittedly one can see more merit in Wordsworth's later poems if one is not blinded by hatred of the man who wrote them. It would be perfectly possible to make an anthology of the poems he wrote after 1810 which would still show him as a major English poet; and also, again as in the case of Yeats, it is quite clear that, however great the differences may be, the early and late poems are all obviously written by the same man, and we gain if we take the whole body of his work as the field of discussion. Mr. Bateson does not think so; he is only interested in the earlier work — indeed the very helpful Chronological Table of Wordsworth's compositions which he gives at the end of the book stops at 1815, as if no one could possibly want to go any further. He will not even allow Miss Edith Batho to say that the post-1815 poems contain 'much that is good, some that is magnificent'. She instances a dozen poems by name, but Mr. Bateson will not have it. There are 'good or goodish lines' in these poems, but with two exceptions they cannot 'possibly be called "magnificent"'. Let us pause for a moment over one of the poems they are arguing about, one that Mr. Bateson would set down as having 'good or goodish' lines: the sonnet *Mutability*:

> From low to high doth dissolution climb,
> And sink from high to low, along a scale
> Of awful notes, whose concord shall not fail;
> A musical but melancholy chime,
> Which they can hear who meddle not with crime,
> Nor avarice, nor over-anxious care.
> Truth fails not; but her outward forms that bear
> The longest date do melt like frosty rime,
> That in the morning whitened hill and plain
> And is no more; drop like the tower sublime
> Of yesterday, which royally did wear
> His crown of weeds, but could not even sustain
> Some casual shout that broke the silent air,
> Or the unimaginable touch of Time.

Here I would come down on Miss Batho's side, if she will have me, and call the poem magnificent. To begin with, it is an extremely interesting treatment of the sonnet form. The normal division into octet and sestet is not so much flouted as allowed a certain ghostly existence in the background (much as Milton treats the prosodic and intellectual traditions of the pastoral in *Lycidas*), and the sonnet is built up by very individual means: it consists of two long sentences, which wind on like the sustained lofty passages of the *Prelude*. This counterpoint between one rhythm and the other is brought to a culmination in the last line with its deliberate clash of rhythms, the iambic beat versus the natural speaking run of the words. The two sentences appear on a first reading not to have much to do with each other, but one soon realizes that the point of the two similes in the second one is to make it cohere with the first: things decay and dissolve whether they are hard-wearing or evanescent; frost takes about twenty minutes to melt if the sun is shining, while a cathedral might take a thousand years to fall down, but really they are just the same because 'dissolution' is like music, and plays all over the scale. Indeed it *is* music, for those who have ears to hear. (Wordsworth often said things were like music when he could not think of any other way of describing them: compare 'the still, sad music of humanity'.)

Another interesting feature of this poem is the counterpoint, another one, between Wordsworth's great skill and his almost equally great lack of skill; no one would deny that the sonnet is built up very powerfully, and yet the individual lines are several times clumsy and weak, and there is more than a hint that he was bothered by the difficulty of finding rhymes, just like a man writing his first sonnet. A man who *meddles with crime* would be, properly speaking, a policeman: he means '*indulge in* crime' but cannot find a way of saying so. On the other hand, as if to show that rhyming comes easily to him, he has deliberately made the job harder for himself by carrying on the 'ime' sound into the second half where he needn't have done; one suspects that he knew all along that a very powerful line was going to end with 'Time' and resolved, quite deliberately, to begin as he meant to go on. I have hardly scratched the surface in these few remarks; it is a wonderfully rich fourteen lines' worth. And there are other late poems as good, and better; *Laodamia*, for instance.

Mention of *Laodamia* leads me to what I really wanted to say about this question of Wordsworth's having dried up. Drying up is a thing that only happens to Romantic poets; Shakespeare and Milton both got better, if anything, as they went on; so did Sophocles; so has a modern poet like Robert Graves. It is the Romantics who either die young, like Shelley, Keats, Dylan Thomas, and Hart Crane, or stop writing, like Coleridge, or go on writing and getting less effective, like — but when we come to fill in that last blank we cannot, I think, use the name of Wordsworth. He ceases to be a Romantic poet, if he ever had been wholly one; his later poetry, when it is good, is not good in a Romantic way (I can't, by the way, define that word, but everyone knows roughly what is meant. What I mean is that, for instance, *The Ancient Mariner* is a Romantic poem and *Laodamia* is not). Wordsworth was, as I say, a psychological poet; his subject was the human mind, and above all his own human mind; this kept him very much apart from the Romantic movement generally, because it drew him in the direction of the analytic and philosophical, which they were not good at. Neither was he for that matter, but it kept him always on the other side of the fence as far as Romanticism was concerned and kept alive sides of his writing that he could use in 'years that bring the philosophic mind'. It was the Romantic part that went wrong, and he knew it at the time. C. S. Lewis once remarked to me: 'The real lesson of the *Prelude* is that Romanticism is not enough', but I don't think I saw what he meant until ten years later.

Another thing that makes Wordsworth's later poems impressive is that in the best of them (by which he has a right to be judged) he did not try to tell lies about himself. His subject was always, in one form or another, the workings of his own mind, and, in spite of his obvious wish not to seem irreligious, that mind was, basically, a pagan and pantheist mind. The poem about James Hogg, which is as late as 1835, is essentially a pagan lament over death; there is no feeling that Wordsworth and his friends are going to meet in a happier state; on the contrary, they are like natural forces which cannot be stayed — when it is time for them to go, they go (like Lucy, we recall, who died as soon as Nature's 'work was done' with her):

> Like clouds that rake the mountain-summits,
> Or waves that own no curbing hand,
> How fast has brother followed brother,
> From sunshine to the sunless land!

'They are all gone into the world of' — darkness, in this pagan document, not light. *Laodamia*, again, is moving because of the peculiar kind of hell that Wordsworth inhabited during his

G

declining years; Laodamia, like Annette, was too much in love to behave sensibly, and Protesilaus-Wordsworth has to lecture her and remind her that 'the gods approve The depth, and not the tumult, of the soul'; she was silly enough to want a kiss, although he was only made of air. To pay her out for this the 'just Gods whom no weak pity moved' sent her to dwell in Hades; the surface meaning of the words is that they were right, but the last stanza shows that the trees didn't think so — a pretty certain indication that Wordsworth didn't either, because after all the trees were Nature. The general implication is that he had decided to obey the obvious dictates of reason and respectability, because the years had brought the philosophic mind, but that he was sorry about it in a way that he could only express in poetry. He gives a note to explain that the story of the trees comes from Pliny; this is defensive, because of course it is exactly the kind of story he would like to have made up.

Wordsworth's situation in later life, altogether, is rather similar to that of the hero of one of his early poems, the Farmer of Tilsbury Vale. This worthy man, as Wordsworth delights to recount, bilked his creditors and flitted to London; unfortunately when he got there he was a bit out of his element because he was in a city and not close to Nature, so that the end of the poem is rather touching: Wordsworth hopes that at least he will be near grass and trees in the cemetery. This queer little poem has a lot of essential Wordsworthian feeling in it; the old man who in earlier days had 'got away with it', but is now stranded a long way from the sources of his life, with no chance of getting back to them before he dies, is a figure he was later to embody in his own person, so that one almost wonders how far this acute self-analyst was deliberately prophesying.

I think, then, that the earlier and later poetry of Wordsworth are on the whole very homogeneous, and the main thing is to provide some ordinary clear-cut literary criticism of the whole body of work. And here one remembers a remark made by Ezra

Pound: 'Wordsworth was only half aware of the problems of writing.' Like many of Pound's asides, this points very accurately to a body of considerable truths. Wordsworth was uneasily aware that things are very difficult for a poet who has an original subject-matter; he said that a great and original poet has to create the taste by which his own poetry can be understood; and he drew a lot of attention to himself by issuing the *Lyrical Ballads* with a fighting preface about the language of poetry. Unfortunately, that squib fizzled out, because the arguments were muddled at the crucial points, and also because the best poems in the book were Coleridge's *Ancient Mariner*, which (as far as its poetic method goes) is simply a piece of late eighteenth-century ballad-making in the tradition of Percy's *Reliques*, and *Tintern Abbey*, which has nothing to do with the theories at all. In fact Wordsworth failed from first to last to clothe his subject-matter in forms which matched it in originality; the blank-verse essay was an eighteenth-century form, the formal ode went back to Gray, and through him to Dryden and Cowley; the ballads and lyric measures were already there in the tradition which he took over, and all he did was to push some of these things a little further than they had yet been taken (there is, after all, nothing *quite* like *Peter Bell* in previous English poetry — or subsequent for that matter). This had the effect of masking Wordsworth's tremendous originality and making a lot of his poems read like botched attempts at something his readers were already familiar with — witness the astonishment of nearly all contemporary critics that any major poet could descend to the utter dead-level of the *Excursion*. In a sense they were right; the manner of Young and Akenside, however strengthened, was the wrong vehicle for what he proposed to do.

In fact Wordsworth's choice of form and his ear for tone let him down with monotonous regularity. Many of the anecdotes in *Lyrical Ballads*, if they had been told simply in prose, would have been like Chekov stories; perhaps it was too early for that, and prose fiction was not yet sophisticated enough to carry that kind of tremendous simplicity, but still the choice he actually did make was an unfortunate one. The *Prelude*, again, is a gigantic misalliance of form to content; one can only speculate on what form would have suited it better, but (noticing that the best passages, which are so easily detachable, are usually between fifty and a hundred lines long) we might say, perhaps, that if Wordsworth had only had the inventive ability he ought to have invented a form rather similar to, say, Rilke's *Duino Elegies*. It is only in the sonnets that one feels entirely free of the clash between matter and technique; he tells us that he started to write them after having Milton's sonnets read to him; and the implied criticism of Milton's sonnets in Wordsworth's is excellent. It shows that he had understood them to their depths. (I don't mean 'In his hand The thing became a trumpet'; I mean the way he sympathetically reproduces Milton's tone of voice underneath his own; it shows he was a good critic of literature — a better one, in my opinion, than Coleridge.)

Why was this? Why could Wordsworth never get this important question settled? I think the reason is two-fold. In the first place, he lacked a really helpful literary tradition; what he found to his hand was good, better than a poet has today, but it was not what he needed; and secondly, there was the all-important question of an audience. Let us go back to Mr. Bateson for a moment.

'Wordsworth,' he tells us, 'found it hard to say who it was exactly he wrote his poems for.' In his early days he was mainly addressing a small audience whom he knew personally; and he addressed them in the literal sense by reading his work aloud. He composed aloud, usually in the open air, and always thought of his poetry as being rather like a musical score, that does not come to life until it is *performed*. (Mr. Bateson makes a great point of this, but I thought it was true of all poets. Surely nobody wants his poetry to be read silently? I would go further and say that any writing that has any artistic pretensions, be it oratory, fiction, verse, even conversationally-styled criticism like this piece I am writing, needs the voice before it comes to anything.) At any rate, Wordsworth needed this expectant audience and at one time had a fairly large circle of interested people to whom he was in the habit of reading his work (Mr. Bateson names them on p. 195). Then the rot set in:

> Unfortunately, as he grew older, Wordsworth began to take this intimate inner public too much for granted and to concern himself more and more with the reading public in general. The way to reach this outer public created a difficult technical problem. How could the spoken voice be transposed into the non-spoken voice of the printed page? . . . In the end it was the Wordsworthians who gradually taught the upper middle class how to read Wordsworth. Their eulogies and commentaries bridged a gap that was too wide for Wordsworth to make himself heard across orally.

I am sure this is the heart of the problem. I see it rather differently from Mr. Bateson, because he thinks of it as a specific concrete question of writing for a silently reading public when you have been used to an *audience*. That is an idea that naturally follows from his belief that Wordsworth was peculiar among poets in writing for the voice. As I do not (and never can) believe any such thing, I naturally see it as the universal problem of how to write for the faceless 'general reader'. But I am sure something of the kind was going on.

Wordsworth is indeed a baffling poet to get hold of. He was original and hidebound; acute and stupid; delicate and clumsy. Probably the key to all these contradictions lies in the character of the man. Certainly the poems, as they stand, are full of contradictions; no wonder they have become a problem-hunter's paradise. No wonder either that his work should have received so little literary criticism. Even more than Yeats, he is a poet about whom the simplest statement is likely to be misunderstood. Poor Mr. Bateson, for instance, cannot even get his book sensibly reviewed; a writer in one of the Sunday papers could not get down to business at all because of his amazement at Mr. Bateson's assertion that Wordsworth experienced, and strongly repressed, a love for Dorothy which was not quite a brother's love. Yet every perceptive reader has always noted that something of the sort must have been operative ever since Coleridge guessed that 'Lucy' was Dorothy.

In the reabsorption of Romantic poetry Wordsworth is the lump of gristle that will be digested last. That is why I am glad Mr. Bateson has written this book.

(1954)

'A STRANGER AND AFRAID'

NOTES ON FOUR VICTORIAN POETS

I, a stranger and afraid
In a world I never made.
— A. E. Housman

IT did not, after all, take the Victorians long to get their own back. The debunking period, looking back on it now, seems to have been very short; really only a few years before and after the first war. That short-lived *régime* was scarcely established before the palace revolutions began; naturally, for how *could* people go on accepting (for instance) the idea that Lytton Strachey had any right to make fun of someone like A. H. Clough? The smaller man making fun of the larger is a spectacle that people are bound to tire of; particularly as Strachey couldn't really find anything funny to say about Clough except that as a boy at Rugby he had had weak ankles, so that every time he makes an appearance, in the essay on Florence Nightingale, he has to be balanced on his weak ankles to remind us that he was a Victorian and therefore *must* have been silly. In fact, of course, Clough's sense of irony was finer than Strachey's, so that the impossible situation arose not merely of the smaller man mocking the larger, but of the less subtle ironist being ironic about the keener one. I must not go on about Strachey; it is flogging a dead horse. But to think about the Victorians is, nowadays, to be reminded of how completely the attack on them has crumbled, and Strachey remains the type-figure of a kind of sensibility and attitude that went out of date with lightning speed.

Among the things the Victorians left us was a very rich mass of poetry; I want to put down a few random reflections on it, starting from a central point. The central point is about their relationship to their public, a subject we are all tired of, but which seems to me the key to understanding the position of the Victorian poet.

The essential history of Victorian poetry, to my mind, is that they made a very necessary and laudable effort to escape from the small compound that poets had always inhabited, and that it proved impossible, so that they had to go back. Poetry had always had a small audience, but it must have seemed to them that this exclusiveness was not essential, but only incidental, only caused by physical circumstances. Chaucer had a small public because his poems had to circulate in manuscript; Shakespeare had one because not enough people were literate; Pope because his work was bound up with a certain way of looking at things which was shared only by people in a certain kind of society. But now the old centralization had broken up, printing was easy and cheap, most people could read — surely there was a need for a wider diffusion of poetry, and surely it was a poet's duty to write for a wide audience.

I do not say that they actually *phrased* it like this. But that was, quite obviously, the psychology of the thing. There was no longer any physical reason why a large public should not read contemporary English poetry, and, until the public had been proved guilty, it had to be treated as innocent, and assumed to be a fit audience, though many.

We all know what happened. By the end of the century it was 'art for art's sake, and keep the public out'. The experiment had worked out so disastrously that the typical 'serious' writer of the year 1900 had no request to make of the larger public other than that they should leave him alone. Martin Tupper made a comfortable living, between five and eight hundred a year, out of *Proverbial Philosophy*, over quite a long period, and if he had received his royalties on the enormous pirated American editions he would actually have been a rich man. 'God has blessed my writings to millions of the human race,' he said. But forty years later even very small poets, men with no more talent than Tupper, were proposing to themselves an altogether different ideal; that of being read by fewer and fewer people. This tradition has persisted; Yeats, in the Preface to his *Last Poems*, speaks of being content with an audience as numerous as that which attended the first night of *Comus*. It is a bitter wisdom.

But wisdom, I think, it is. Obviously a large number of people can enjoy verse, just as any tradesman can do simple arithmetic. But the tradesman cannot understand higher mathematics; only a few people are able to do that, and they are first born with the right kind of brain, and later trained in the right way. I should say that the number of people able to read poetry, as it should be read, is about equal to the number of mathematicians; there are usually a few thousand. I am not silly enough to think that the others ought not to read poetry at all; obviously they will get a lot out of it, and it will be good for them. But it is the very small number of able, discriminating readers who must constitute the public for new poetry. They are the point at which communication and exchange become possible, the point at which growth can be seen. The others will read Martin Tupper and his modern counter-parts. They will be pleased, and to a great extent instructed, by these authors; but in this essay we are talking about poetry as an art, not as a social service.

I think this is a fairer way of putting it than to accuse Tennyson and Browning of selling out, which is the usual charge. The psychological pressure on them was simply too great. It had not yet been proved that an audience the size of, say, Wyatt's or Jonson's was the best — the best because it provided the poet with a living, tangible audience, with whom some human interplay was possible — and until it had, they could not assume it. Tennyson and Browning are, in fact, something like martyrs; they each devoted a lifetime to trying the impossible, because it was what a sensible man would naturally do in their situation. They both shut themselves out of 'the real right place', the control tower, and naturally could not get any work done in the street. Mr. J. B. Priestley, complaining in a recent article about the thin time writers are having, and the decline in their prestige, said, 'Tennyson

was there with Gladstone in a way in which Mr. Eliot is not
here with Winston Churchill,' but of course that is just what
helps Mr. Eliot; it is the only respect in which his job is easier than
Tennyson's. Everyone who visits the Eastern European Communist countries remarks on how similar they are, in some
respects, to Victorian England; the same materialistic optimism,
the belief that a millennium will arise of its own accord when once
enough material progress has been made, produces the same
official policy: the idea that art should be accessible to everyone.
Communist theory would not permit any touch of the esoteric,
the arcane, in art because of its basic assumption that what all
can't have, no one must: Victorian self-confidence made a similar
demand. (In Victorian England it was enforced not by an official-
dom, but by respectable bourgeois opinion, which was easier to
defy.) The effect of this on the poets of its own day was to inter-
cept the two most original of them, and to turn them back at the
boundaries of greatness.

Is this unbearably pessimistic? — will it, even, be called arro-
gant? But I am only one among so many who have been forced
to realize it. And in the end we must not make this the most
important question. A contemporary poet, Randall Jarrell, has
this passage in his *Poetry and the Age*:

> People always ask: *For whom does the poet write?* He needs only to
> answer, *For whom do you do good? Are you kind to your daughter
> because in the end someone will pay you for being?* . . . The poet writes
> his poem for its own sake, for the sake of that order of things in
> which the poem takes the place that has awaited it.

The trouble with a poet who is too uneasily aware of the effort
to form a relationship with a public he cannot see or feel is that he
is in just the position of being kind to his daughter because he will
be paid for it. Tennyson fell into this state; and because he was the
major figure who might have given a lead, the whole tribe found
themselves in the same difficulty; but there was no need for it to
have happened. I think it arguable that if Arthur Hallam had lived,

Tennyson would not have been stricken with the inner loneliness that led him to conform. Hallam saw the whole situation, and described it accurately in his review of Tennyson's poems in *The Englishman's Magazine* in 1831. The larger public, he is pointing out, will never care for poetry unless it is diluted.

> Since this demand on the reader for activity, when he wants to peruse his author in a luxurious passiveness, is the very thing that moves his bile, it is obvious that those writers will always be popular who require the least degree of exertion. Hence, whatever is mixed up with art, and appears under its semblance, is always more favourably regarded than art free and unalloyed. Hence, half the fashionable poems in the world are mere rhetoric and half the remainder are, perhaps, not liked by the generality for their substantial merits.

Hallam put his finger on it there. But to have helped Tennyson through a lifetime of creation, he would have had to survive; and this duty, unfortunately, he neglected.

This, as I say, seems to me a fairer way of putting it than to say that Tennyson and Browning just deserted the colours. Mr. David Daiches, in *Poetry and the Modern World* (1940), seems to me to condemn them too harshly, as if they had *wanted* to be second-rate.

> The aim of Tennyson, as he saw it, was to come to terms with his age: he may not have achieved his aim completely or comfortably, but there can be little doubt that it *was* his aim, as it was Browning's. The optimism of Browning and the pessimism of Tennyson . . . are both products of this aim: the former tried to achieve it by breeziness and ruggedness, the latter by worry, morality, and (alternatively) choicely cadenced hysteria.

The age seems, at any rate, to have left them a fairly free hand if it was possible to come to terms with it by being either optimistic or pessimistic, either rugged or 'choicely cadenced'; but in any case the charge against these poets is that they sold out. It is wrong to agree too much with one's age, and fatal if that age is the age of Victoria. Three years after Mr. Daiches's book, Mr. Cyril Connolly, in his essay '1843', confirmed the diagnosis:

> Tennyson, our greatest poet of the last hundred years, might have been one of the greatest poets of the world if he had listened to his instinct alone, if he had not permitted his reason to enforce the doctrines of the day, not felt it his duty to be a philosopher-bard, a State-mouthpiece, rather than a wild and sensual voice of protest, a dying swan.

Yes, Tennyson has that kind of power; for a few hours after reading him you are ready to overrate him wildly; he has his own field of force, and I would not trust anyone's taste who did not have to tug against it. To get rid of the enchantment, of course, it is only necessary to open some major poet; a few lines of Shakespeare or Milton, and Tennyson is back where he usually lives. Mr. Connolly, in making the obviously absurd claim that Tennyson was the greatest poet of the last hundred years (a glance at either Yeats or Hopkins would have been sufficient to see *that* idea off) was actually expressing, very clearly, the mood we all know: Tennyson-dazzle, producing blindness to the real nature of poetry.

Browning is a similar, though differently situated, figure. His genuflexion to Victorian society was to step into the rôle of its Difficult Poet (there always has to be one). He pleased the Browning Societies, and made deliciously quotable remarks on the lines of, 'There was a time when God and Robert Browning knew what that poem meant: now only God knows', and so forth. He roughened the surface of his verse as a means of disguising the essential simplicity of its content; and this is the clue to why, when roughness had its vogue some thirty years after his death, there was no upward swing in his reputation; everyone was able to see, by that time, that 'Irks care the crop-full bird? Frets doubt the maw-crammed beast?' is a needlessly hard way of saying 'Animals don't worry when they have enough to eat.' Or, as Dr. Leavis put it, 'the characteristic corrugation of his surface is merely superficial, and not the expression of a complex sensibility'. Leaving aside for a moment the question of whether it is always a *sine quâ non* for a poet to have a complex sensibility, it is certainly true that unless he has one he should not make obvious claims in that direction, by means of the texture of his verse. In this respect Browning is not unlike Auden, another poet not liked by Dr. Leavis. They are both given to mystification that does not go deep; when Auden is difficult, it is often a result of mere carelessness, and because, from the start, he had an uncritically admiring public who did not insist on being treated fairly.

> Sir, no man's enemy, forgiving all,
> But will his negative inversion be prodigal.

I know this can be read as 'forgiving all but the negative inversion of will', but if so, why not punctuate intelligibly? And why, in any case, is God, who is addressed with the Hopkinsian 'Sir', asked to be prodigal? It does not seem to fit in with anything in the rest of the poem.

When, on the other hand, Auden *wants* to be understood, he is the plainest poet imaginable.

> Hunger allows no choice
> To citizens or the police;
> We must love one another or die.

In the same way, Browning, when he *wants* to be understood, can drop the clowning.

> Never the time and the place
> And the loved one all together

— it could hardly be more straightforward.[1]

Part of Browning's oddity comes from his obsession with technique, which is something he shares with Tennyson. Neither of them, one feels, felt quite secure about the status of the poet in an

---

[1] Both are about equally remote from the Tennysonian sublime of — for instance —

> His heavy-shotted hammock-shroud
> Drops in his vast and wandering grave.

age that was increasingly preoccupied with the novel, and part of their answer (an uneasy one) was to write a great deal in quantity, and put — each in his own way — a higher and higher gloss on the surface. The more Tennyson planed his verses to smoothness, the more Browning chipped his to roughness. Browning had a keen eye for exotic detail, and this helped him to fashion delightful little oddments to stick on to his poems like gargoyles. His technique is really remarkable; there is too much of it, of course, so that in the end it defeats its own object, and this makes him a poet to be read a few pages at a time rather than in bulk; but the virtuosity cannot be denied. He began, in *Pauline* (published in 1833, but written a couple of years earlier), as a kind of pendant or dinghy of second-generation romanticism, very much influenced by Shelley. But already, in this kind of thing, he has his own manner under the borrowed one; it is Browning, not Shelley, that we recognize:

> Thou wilt remember one warm morn when winter
> Crept aged from the earth, and spring's first breath
> Blew soft from the moist hills; the black-thorn boughs,
> So dark in the bare wood, when glistening
> In the sunshine were white with coming buds,
> Like the bright side of a sorrow, and the banks
> Had violets opening from sleep like eyes.
> I walked with thee who knew'st not a deep shame
> Lurked beneath smiles and careless words which sought
> To hide it till they wandered and were mute,
> As we stood listening on a sunny mound
> To the wind murmuring in the damp copse,
> Like heavy breathings of some hidden thing
> Betrayed by sleep; until the feeling rushed
> That I was low indeed, yet not so low
> As to endure the calmness of thine eyes;
> And so I told thee all, while the cool breast
> I leaned on altered not its quiet beating.

The first assays of young poets have their own charm, and I find this very delightful; he has picked up Shelley's manner so cleverly and yet his own keeps breaking through, especially in the entirely un-Shelleyan robustness that lurks about; it is impossible to feel that the young man in the story had really done anything so very low. And his leaning on her cool breast is an endearing touch of absurdity, as in Daisy Ashford. I like *Pauline*.

In the mature Browning there is always an *abandon*, a glittering profusion of technique which, even in a poem otherwise not worth much, makes one rub one's eyes.

> I could favour you with sundry touches
> Of the paint-smutches with which the Duchess
> Heightened the mellowness of her cheek's yellowness
> (To get on faster) till at last her
> Cheek grew to be one master-plaster
> Of mucus and fucus from mere use of ceruse:
> In short, she grew from scalp to udder
> Just the object to make you shudder.

This is like Auden's

> Tempting to mortals in the fancy of half-concerned
> Gods in the sky, of a bored Thunderer who turned
> From the Troy-centred grief to
> Watch the Hippemolgoi drink their milk,
>
> And how plausible from his look-point: we may well
> Shake a weak fist one day at this vision, but the spell
> Of high places will haunt us
> Long after our jaunt has declined,
>
> As soon it must, to the hard ground. Where six foot is tall,
> Good-manners will ask easy riddles like 'Why are all
> The rowdiest marches and the
> Most venomous iambics composed
>
> By lame clergymen?' will tell no tales which end in worse
> Disaster than that of the tipsy poet who cursed
> A baby for whom later
> He came to sigh — so we were taught
>
> Before the Greater Engines came and the police
> Who go with them.

The Browning (from *The Flight of the Duchess*) has the same rather self-congratulatory muscle-play as the Auden (from *Ode to Gaea*); both poets are using their technique to pull a fast one on the reader; but in Browning's case one feels that it is done more gracefully. The clowning is justified by the contemptuous nature of the subject-matter, whereas the lines from Auden have the air of saying something very impressive — yet after the most attentive reading one can't be sure whether, for instance, 'in' is not a misprint for 'is' in the first line (in copying the passage out, by the way, I had to correct one misprint). What makes such verse depressing is the large gesturing, the air of quick-wittedness and breadth of reference, which seems to have nothing deeply-felt at its centre.

Where Auden's cleverness resides largely in his juggling with tone, Browning's is partly honest horseplay with words and partly a very exceptional gift, as I said earlier, for drawing exotic vignettes. This was something he learnt from Shelley, no doubt; Shelley is always giving us things like this:

> I cannot tell my joy, when o'er a lake
> Upon a drooping bough with nightshade twin'd,
> I saw two azure halcyons clinging downward
> And thinning one bright bunch of amber berries,
> With quick long beaks, and in the deep there lay
> Those lovely forms imaged as in a sky.
> (Prometheus Unbound, IV, 78 ff.)

Browning is not often so exotic, but he has the same gift of vivid evocation of an unusual impression made on the senses:

> . . . through the morass
> Where never sound yet was
> Save the dry quick clap of the stork's bill,
> For the air is still, and the water still,
> Where the blue breast of the dipping coot
> Dives under, and all is mute.
> (The Flight of the Duchess.)

In trying to write about Browning, I seem to have done nothing but quote him; but this is in fact how he is to be enjoyed.
His work is a repository of fascinating odds and ends, always
worth rummaging through; it is not great poetry, but only a
man who was, in flashes, and incompletely, a great poet, could
have written it.

HOPKINS

With Hopkins we reach another stage in the relationship of the
Victorian poet to his public; because *his* public consisted solely of
a few friends, just enough to take the edge off his utter solitude.
He worked with the barest minimum of equipment; most of the
things that poets find helpful — travel, variety, admiration,
physical comfort — he did without. He also did without physical
health, being woefully tried by ailments, and without extensive
leisure. To cap it, the friends to whom he showed his verse were
almost entirely useless to him.

He is, indeed, the supremely *deprived* poet, the great do-er without. In his long critical battle with Bridges, he was without
weapons save for what pebbles he could catch up and throw, not
always accurately. He was a David without even a sling. In the
Hopkins–Bridges correspondence, we see modern poetry utterly
defenceless, without any of the armour which two generations of
criticism have since forged for it. His *naïveté* seems touching,
pathetic — for even great artists have their pathetic side, as all men
do. That coarseness of Bridges, that donnish assurance! His all-too-
facile accusation of breaking with tradition! 'We at High Table
know how poetry ought to be written; we learnt it at the fountain-
head, from Spenser and the Greek and Latin classics' — see his
Introduction to D. M. Dolben's poems for his own account of
this — 'and whatever *your* way of writing is, it isn't the Tradition.'
Any undergraduate nowadays could turn the whole argument
inside out. Bridges had a conception of 'tradition' that wouldn't,
really, stand a moment's examination; in fact 'examination' is a

H

very apt word here, for every year our Universities wearily confer B.A.s on third-class candidates who could explain glibly, against the clock — and *do* explain — that the Tradition, for Bridges, so obviously left out much that we pride ourselves on in English poetry; Donne, the late Shakespeare, whole areas of neo-classic verse, for instance; and what of the six centuries during which English poetry tuned itself to non-Mediterranean rhythms, the centuries before Chaucer? 'What ish my Nation? Ish a Villaine, and a Basterd, and a Knaue, and a Rascall. What is my Nation? Who talkes of my Nation?' What a fine patriotic fervour Hopkins might have infused into his answer, if he had only known the patter — the patter that anyone knows today. But he could only stammer his answer — something about 'Pierce-Ploughman', something about Sprung Rhythm.

It amuses me, even now, to see writers on Hopkins still repeating the weary old rigmarole about Sprung Rhythm. It is so obviously a smoke-screen, designed not to illuminate the poetry but to hide it from the coarse prodding forefinger of Bridges. Bridges liked donnish games with metre; his book on Milton's prosody is a perfect example of the kind of criticism that is useless, or positively hampering, to any but the reader who has already reached the stage where he has no need of it. Show him a poem, and let him make what he can of it, and at once the rumble of pejorative terms will begin — 'Oddity', 'Eccentricity', 'Obscurity', all these so great as to 'deny him even a hearing from those who love a continuous literary decorum, and are grown to be impatient of its absence'. But tell him, 'This is a metrical experiment; you might find it interesting. I call it Sprung Rhythm —' that is the strategy for him. But why has it got to be the strategy for *us*?

No, those pages in the Oxford *Hopkins* are just comic material, good for a chuckle or, if we remember the travail that produced them, a wry smile. Some of it, indeed, is the broadest comedy. The explanation culminates, you will remember, with an arithmetical equation, intended to clarify the prosodic nature of the 'curtal-sonnet' to those readers who grasp a thing more clearly if it is put into numbers. In the first edition, this ran:

$$\frac{12}{8} + \frac{9}{2} = \frac{21}{2} = 10\frac{1}{2}$$

In the subsequent editions, the arithmetical blunder was corrected; but without, I submit, making the set-up really more impressive.

It is the same, of course, with the theological apparatus, so faithfully trotted out by the Jesuit critics. The object here is to prove, not that Hopkins naturally expressed a theocentric view of nature — which we should all agree to — but that he was actually a versifier of Thomist doctrine; that he was the Roman Catholic poet *par excellence*, whose poems cannot even be comprehended without a study of his theological reading. This, to be frank, is about on a level with the 'Sprung Rhythm' business. It is merely the understandable and forgivable desire of official Romanism to keep one ahead. The vogue of Hopkins which followed on the publication of his poems in 1918 was, we may suppose, both a delight and a shock to his co-religionists. A delight because it enabled them to drop Francis Thompson as the official Roman Catholic poet of modern times (and it wasn't too soon to get out from under *that* structure) without feeling definitely committed to, say, Chesterton. A shock, because after all it was the opposite camp who welcomed him first, and with a more convincing show of understanding him. As H. M. McLuhan has remarked,

> The Catholic reader comes to Hopkins with a mechanism of sensibility which came off the line in 1850. His sensibility has been unmodified by the impact of Baudelaire, Laforgue, Pound or Eliot. Bloomsbury was at least readied for Hopkins by these and *The Seafarer*. But the Catholic assumes his proprietary manner on the strength of doctrinal affinity alone.

Not that one wants to overstress the dichotomy in Hopkins between 'poet' and 'priest'; nobody would wish to revive the caricature, which some of his early apologists put about in their first impatient zeal, of a Hopkins aching to lead the free and roving life of a poet, forced into another path by his priestly conscience, and writing bitter little poems complaining about it. No; but at the same time there is no need to be equally silly in the opposite direction. Father W. A. M. Peters, for instance, writes very helpfully on most points in his *Gerard Manley Hopkins* (1948), but when he comes to this point he starts hedging like mad. On page 47 he launches out with:

> . . . the painful thing was not that as a priest he was not allowed in conscience to spend time on poetry; he never cared greatly for his own poetry, and would never take the trouble of making fair copies or preserving them from being lost. Bridges did all that for him. Besides, he cared more for his philosophical work than for his poems.

The idea of Hopkins as merely doodling poems in the intervals of earnestly applying himself to theological studies is not one that we can be expected to take seriously. That one of the greatest poets of his century — since Wordsworth, fairly obviously *the* greatest — should have felt obliged, for reasons connected with that same religion that formed his main subject-matter, to mortify himself by claiming not to care about his poetry, by letting it lie about in uncorrected copies, and so on, we may take as an interesting biographical fact. Once we begin, however, to take as our concern the poetry and not the biography, once we begin to let Hopkins's poems speak for themselves, we can hardly continue to repeat this bland stuff about how he thought of his verse as an unimportant hobby, and 'cared more' (in what sense? At what level?) 'for his philosophical work'. *Could* anyone (to ask the simple question) have written these poems if he 'never cared greatly' for his art? It is safer, in these matters, to trust to the poems than to Hopkins's utterances in letters and such-like; and the wonderful poem which Hopkins wrote to apologise to Bridges for not writing better poetry contains, in its sestet, the modest and simple explanation; he doesn't enjoy life enough, is too generally low-spirited, to feel like writing poetry very often:

> Sweet fire the sire of muse, my soul needs this;
> I want the one rapture of an inspiration.
> O then if in my lagging lines you miss
> The roll, the rise, the carol, the creation,
> My winter world, that scarcely breathes that bliss
> Now, yields you, with some sighs, our explanation.

No one could have written *that* who didn't know how to value 'the roll, the rise, the carol, the creation', however casual he was about making fair copies. And Fr. Peters's quite gratuitous pat on the shoulder for Bridges (who 'did all that for him') is also put in its proper light by this poem, which was marked by one of Bridges's pieces of insolence towards Hopkins — the emendation of 'combs' in line 6 to 'moulds', 'having no doubt that G. M. H. would have made some such alteration'. High Table again!

Hopkins, to come back to our thread, is the *defenceless* poet; he knew how to write 'modern poetry', but he didn't know the patter that goes with it. We can do the patter for him, of course, retrospectively; we know that Ambiguity is a good thing, where Bridges would have thought it a bad thing; so that we can point triumphantly to the richer and denser quality that Hopkins can get into his poems by such locutions as

> O, the sots and thralls of lust
> Do in spare hours more thrive than I that spend
> Sir, life upon thy cause.

The sots outpace him in their 'spare' hours — the bits of time they have left over from enjoying themselves, and also the hours in which their lives are *spare* and ascetic: the hours when they 'in a pet of temperance feed on pulse'. (The second of these two is, obviously, the 'head' sense.) Every page has its examples; Bridges saw them, of course, but his idea of commenting on them was merely to include them in the catalogue of Hopkins's 'faults'; 'a reader looking for a verb may find that he has two or three ambiguous monosyllables from which to select, and must be in doubt as to which promises best to give any meaning that he can welcome; and then, after his choice is made, he may be left with some homeless monosyllable still on his hands'. It is this kind of thing that makes one realize how important it is for critics to illustrate their remarks with concrete quotation and analysis; if Bridges had *produced* one of these cases where he found a homeless monosyllable still on his hands, it might soon have struck people that a home could be found for it.

One mustn't, of course, make Hopkins out to have been a good poet in proportion as he needs defending by our kind of patter; often when he is at his most obscure and idiosyncratic, he is at his least interesting. I don't mean 'And to-fro tender tram-beams truckle at the eye'; that is not such a silly line; a candle's beams, seen through narrowed eyes when the light is filtered by the lashes, really look like lines of yellow light; and the nearest thing to these lines that can be found anywhere else is the reflection of street lighting on tram-lines in a wet town night. Hopkins would be more familiar with tram-lines, wet or dry, than we are today; he would also have seen a 'truckle-bed', which ran on castors so as to be pushed under a normal-sized bed. The beams of candle-light go gently to and fro, between the flame and the eye, as gently as a truckle-bed being pushed about. It is not a good line, but it is not absurd, to my mind. The kind of thing I mean is this:

> Only what word
> Wisest my heart breeds dark heaven's baffling ban
> Bars or hell's pell thwarts. This to hoard unheard,
> Heard unheeded, leaves me a lonely began.

The first sentence is all right; it is not even idiosyncratic, except that the adjective 'wisest' is placed after its noun, for which there is plenty of justification. It is the word 'began' that pushes the thing over the edge. Bridges, who must have had access to a dialect dictionary, did not know what it meant, so presumably it is not some special word, but merely a strained use of the preterite of 'begin'. 'Leaves me a lonely (one who only) began', Bridges explains, no doubt rightly; but this sort of thing is not really justifiable; English will do most things without being frog-marched about in this way. It is necessary to point frankly to these things even at the risk of being taken to agree with those people who object to *every* instance, in *every* poem, of the sort of vitality that coins new forms of existing words; the freedom to do this was one of Hopkins's legacies to contemporary poetry, and often the same people who object to Hopkins also protest when, for instance, Dylan Thomas uses the expression 'the heron-priested shore'. To me it is natural enough that, if a ship can be 'manned', *i.e.* provided with men, a shore can be 'priested', *i.e.* provided with priests, and that the herons, standing motionless and lonely at intervals on the shore, are the priests in question. Shakespeare could use 'woman'd', in the sense of 'accompanied by a woman'; Hopkins merely asserted the right to restore this kind of gram-matical fluidity.

In fact, we can soon see that where Hopkins is bad, he is so not because of the occasional extravagances into which he is led by his own unique poetic method, but because of his failures to employ that method consistently. He wrote about as many bad poems as good ones; it is a fact that the worst poems, or patches of poems, are often written by the best poets (cf. Wordsworth, Keats, Shakespeare), and Hopkins's bad poems are of almost every kind, ranging from the Newboltian jingoistic thump-thump of 'What shall I do for the land that bred me', through the patchiness — now good, now terrible — of 'The Loss of the Eurydice', to the more sophisticated badness of a poem like 'Inversnaid', which I had better quote:

> This darksome burn, horseback brown,
> His rollrock highroad roaring down,
> In coop and in comb the fleece of his foam
> Flutes and low to the lake falls home.

A windpuff-bonnet of fawn-froth
Turns and twindles over the broth
Of a pool so pitchblack, fell-frowning,
It rounds and rounds Despair to drowning.

Degged with dew, dappled with dew
Are the groins of the braes that the brook treads through,
Wiry heathpacks, flitches of fern,
And the beadbonny ash that sits over the burn.

What would the world be, once bereft
Of wet and of wildness? Let them be left,
O let them be left, wildness and wet;
Long live the weeds and the wilderness yet.

This is bad because of the blurred effect caused by smearing one technique over the top of another. There are a few felicitous touches in Hopkins's unique manner, particularly in the first two stanzas: 'A windpuff-bonnet of fawn-froth' is unforgettable, as an instance of his power to brood over some detail of external nature until he has worked out *exactly* how to translate its impression into language; and 'Wiry heathpacks' is almost as good. But already we are aware of a slight uneasiness, almost physical, a kind of seasickness produced by the awkward rolling gait of the poem. The rhythm is conventional — in, for instance, the last two lines of the first stanza — and this conventionality is fighting against the originality of the diction. In stanza 3 we get the give-away completely with the mechanical jolting of the second line, and with the last line, 'And the beadbonny ash that sits over the burn', the thing falls to pieces altogether. That line belongs in a different kind of poem; it would fit naturally into 'Little Boy Blue, come blow up your horn', and as such would be a satisfactory line in a satisfactory poem; but jammed side by side with lines that have the unique Hopkinsian claim to be 'counter, original, spare, strange', it jars fearfully. Finally, as if he knew when he was beaten, Hopkins just stuck down any old stuff that came into his head to make the last stanza. It is like something out of a school magazine.

These strictures do not seriously affect Hopkins; one makes them, not by way of reducing his status, but merely to get his achievement into clearer focus. When a man in continual bad health, overburdened with duties, and fighting permanent scruples about giving time to his art in the first place — when such a man is also an *ambitious* poet, there are bound to be a lot of outright failures and half-successes. And Hopkins *was* ambitious; it is almost the most important fact about his poetry. He was always trying to see how near he could get to the impossible. Language is a very useful tool, but it is a limited one; for instance, it is hardly any use at all in describing physical objects and processes. If you were talking to some African bush pigmy who had never seen a staircase, for instance, you would not waste time trying to *describe* a staircase in words, however well you knew his language; you would get a pencil and the back of an envelope and draw it for him. Similarly with a pair of skates or a bicycle. Notice how often, in everyday conversation, one resorts to gesture when describing physical entities — holding up one hand to represent the wall the bus nearly ran into, etc. If you saw a kestrel flying, would it occur to you to try to describe it by words *alone*? No — but Hopkins delights in setting himself this task; he insists on telling us what the Falcon looked like

>   in his riding
> Of the rolling underneath him steady air, and striding
> High there, how he rung upon the rein of a wimpling wing
> In his ecstasy! Then off, off forth on swing,
> As a skate's heel sweeps smooth on a bow-bend: the hurl and gliding
> Rebuffed the big wind.

Without proposing to add to the mountain of commentary that this poem has called into being, I want simply to point out that it is, among other things, a virtuoso exercise in making language do something for which it is not, ultimately, fitted. Part of the pleasure we get from reading 'The Windhover' is, in fact, a re-fined and heightened version of the pleasure it gives some people, at any rate, to see unlikely materials coerced by ingenuity; you can always attract sight-seers with a life-size statue of Sir W. Churchill done in sea-weed, or a working scale model of Stephenson's 'Rocket' made of ground rice. The Victorians were especially fond of this kind of exercise, and I hope it does not sound fanciful if I say that Hopkins, in this kind of poem, is linked with this 'Victorianism' as firmly as he is linked with the pioneering spirit of modernism in literature, which in his day was just beginning to stir. An expert in Victoriana, writing in *The Times Literary Supplement* (October 6, 1950), reminded us of the lengths these people could go to:

> . . . trophies were made of shells, feathers, seeds, acorns and bones; the Royal Family was embroidered in human hair, moss was made from wool and wool from moss, crinoline metal was twisted into work-baskets, the Bay of Naples was depicted in glue and sand, settees were made from the horns of German stags, roses were cut out of leather, sandwiches and bisected hard-boiled eggs were reproduced in life-like wax to sit beneath domes of glass. In imaginative power and thorough-going ugliness these gew-gaws far surpassed the wildest efforts of the Surrealists.

Hopkins thought 'The Windhover' his best poem, but I have to admit that to me it is a little too close to the Bay of Naples in glue and sand; Rayner Heppenstall recalls I. A. Richards reading it 'with circular planings of the hand', which seems an apt detail to mention here; he was re-translating this description into its natural medium, a visual one.

I prefer Hopkins when he is dealing with his central subject-matter. And this subject-matter is actually quite simple. He was a priest whose life was dedicated to God and who happened at the same time to be hypersensitive to sensory impressions. His responsiveness to external nature was so blissful and so intensely developed that but for his religious vocation, it would undoubtedly have been the mainspring of his life. (As a youth he was in contact with Pater, which might amount to anything or nothing.) As it was, this responsiveness was challenged by an equally intense volume of religious feeling. When I say 'challenged', I don't mean that there was any tragic conflict between them, but simply that they were the two chief things in his consciousness, and naturally now one, now the other, was uppermost.

The bridge, of course, was that it was God who created Nature, so that to adore Nature was to adore God, which was not only delightful but an actual duty; furthermore, it was in this activity that man fulfilled himself and rose to his highest level, so that

> This Jack, joke, poor potsherd, patch, matchwood, immortal diamond
> Is immortal diamond.

That Hopkins sometimes chafed at his life is a fact that merely puts him in the same category as the rest of humanity. His terrible cry for the relief of his spiritual drought — the sonnet that ends 'send my roots rain' — is, after all, accompanied on the same page by the poem celebrating a saint who did nothing all his life but wait in patience.

> Yet God (that hews mountain and continent,
> Earth, all, out; who, with trickling increment
> Veins violets and tall trees makes more and more)
> Could crowd career with conquest while there went
> Those years and years by of world without event
> That in Majorca Alfonso watched the door.

Hopkins as the deprived poet, as the poet utterly lacking in encouragement, did the one thing that no other poet of his time was able to do: he produced, suddenly, a new style that made all other available methods seem obsolete. The story is one of the most purely astonishing in the history of any of the arts, and as such it is known to everyone; how, on entering the Society of Jesus, he thought of himself as abandoning his poetic vocation, and destroyed most of his work; how his superiors in the Order permitted, or encouraged, him to resume it; and how, some seven

years later, he sat down to write on the news of a sea-tragedy that
moved him, and suddenly, astonishingly, the new poetry flowed
out.

> Over again I feel thy finger and find thee.

The first stanza of *The Wreck of the Deutschland* is the most *surprising* — not to say surprised — piece of English verse ever
written. Without knowing it, this lonely, ailing young priest had
gestated a new poetry, and now it was delivered. When this happened, Hopkins was thirty-one. Writing in the same year of my
own life, I feel (if a personal note is not too obtrusive here) impelled to say, as a writer of verse myself, that I understand something of what he felt; enough, at least, to feel the reverence that is
his due.

HOUSMAN

I have been expecting — but not, so far, seeing — a resurgence
of interest in Housman; if not as a poet, then at least as a case-
history. After all, he was, in his day, almost alone in facing a problem which is nowadays faced by quite a number of people: the
problem of how to combine the two functions of poet and professor. If we read 'literary artist of any kind' for 'poet', and
'academic teacher of any kind' for 'professor', we have a situation
that is very much of our time; both in England and America, the
universities are coming to provide a shelter for writers which
saves them from having to be schoolteachers or ad. men — though
there is still no tendency, in this country at any rate, for a university to employ a poet *because* he is a poet. He gets the job first, in
the normal way, and then shyly produces his poems. It is one
illustration of the way the universities have taken over some of the
social functions of the Church; in the seventeenth century a lot of
the best poets were parsons, because the Church was then what
the university is today — a large, impersonal, non-profit-making
organization, securely established, and able to use men of diverse
talents in diverse ways.

However, a modern university teacher is not in the same position as a seventeenth-century clergyman. He has more work to do, for one thing; and, on the whole, harder work. Furthermore, he is under pressures which none of his predecessors knew. When his academic colleagues are not sneering at him for being literary, his literary friends are sneering at him for being academic, and both groups are very good at sneering. Worst of all, he is trying to serve two gods at once, and haunted by the fear that he will, in the end, satisfy neither. As an artist, he needs *luxe, calme, volupté, ordre,* and *beauté,* and all the university can supply him with (perhaps, fortunately) is *ordre* and a limited amount of *calme.* It is not an accident that, until very recent times, no don except Lewis Carroll (and, would one add, Pater?) ever wrote a work of imaginative literature that had enough vitality to keep it alive.

Housman side-stepped these problems, partly by luck and partly by giving in to them. When I say 'luck', I mean that his extraordinary talent for emending Latin texts brought him, in early middle life, a Cambridge chair which seems to have involved no very arduous duties. When I say 'giving in' I mean that Housman made no attempt to do two things at once. He merely assimilated the poet in him to the professor. The smallness of his output, the narrowness of his range, the elaborate pains he took to safeguard the text from misprints (as if he were one of his own dead authors), are all academic characteristics. So was his inability, or refusal, to develop, to admit any new light, to *move* in any direction.

I must elaborate this last point a little. Housman's major faults as a poet — the things that kept him a *minor* poet — are (*a*) the immature and commonplace nature of his subject-matter, all self-pity and grumbling; (*b*) the lack of any development. Although he wrote poems over a period of some forty years, it is oddly true that if one shuffled them, and had only internal evidence to go by, one would never recover the original order. That is why I feel

justified in discussing him among 'Victorian' poets, in spite of his
going on writing until well into my own lifetime. The last poems
he wrote are no different from the first; that is, they exhibit faults
(*a*) and (*b*) above.

Now this is such an extraordinary thing — for after all it is
human to develop, and we usually do so whether we wish to or
not — that one has to ask the reason for it. I have already called it
an *academic* characteristic; and, unfortunately, the evidence seems
to bear me out. There is something about the academic atmosphere that fosters habit, repetition, getting set in one's ways.
Everything is so permanent. Perhaps all institutions do this; certainly the Army and the Church have both been accused of it.
And of course a professor is like a colonel or an archdeacon in one
respect: most of his work consists of doing the same thing over
and over again. When Housman had finished taking one class
through Propertius, there would be another waiting to begin.
When he had edited one piece by Manilius, he started on another
one just like it.

Now Housman can hardly be blamed for succumbing to this
petrification. If it is true that even the strongest minds go down,
how could he resist? For his was not, in any broad sense, a strong
mind. His stock of ideas was tiny, his human responsiveness, after
early life, almost nil; his general intelligence, poor. (Cite *one* interesting remark that Housman made on any general topic.) His
getting himself ploughed in Greats was good strategy; it enabled
him to claim not to have been trying; and there is no evidence
that he would have done well if he *had* tried. Philosophy was
obviously alien ground to him. If the tendency of Cambridge was
to shut him off from life, it must be said that he collaborated to the
full. He spared no pains to turn himself into the solitary, life-
resisting, formidable figure of the anecdotes. The banked-up fires
exploded in two directions only; his poems, and his savage
baiting of other scholars who did not conform to his standards of
accuracy.

I have often thought that the bitterness with which Housman attacked his classical colleagues was, to some extent, compensatory. It is a common characteristic of men who have a special, and narrow, gift that they are harshly critical of anyone who tries to compete with them. Housman's gift of emendation was the product partly of industry and partly of the hypersensitive quality of his ear. (Poets are often good at emendation; there is an emendation of Milton's in the received text of the *Bacchae* of Euripides.) It was, in other words, largely a *knack*. He knew a lot of Latin, and he had a knack of making a special use of what he knew. It was a gift, like his poetry. And neither gift had much to do with the ordinary functions of the intelligence. Housman was not a very intelligent man; his poetry proves it. His poetry also proves that he was supremely, if narrowly, gifted.

These remarks may seem merely provoking, but I think they can be proved. After all, a very gifted poet *can* be a stupid man; his stupidity will keep him a minor poet, but it will not spoil his gift. And a great classical scholar can be stupid too, off his own ground. Bentley, who is usually named as Housman's only superior, has left us detailed proof of his imbecility, in his emendations of *Paradise Lost*. What, then, is the moral?

The moral is, if you are going to be an academic poet, *be stupid*. Dig in, refuse to grow, and cultivate your most specialized talent. Then both sides will respect you. Housman was fantastically overpraised, in his lifetime and since, by his fellow academics, because he offers a justification of the donnish way of life. But for the young writer, employed at a university, he is the *memento mori*. The dead hand of academicism, which kills everything it touches, lay heavily on his exquisite gift. He rejected life, and life certainly had its own back on his poetry, which never gets free of a certain triviality, a certain pettiness and lack of emotional breadth. Even when he re-works a poem by a much better poet, he dares not follow his guide out into the open; I am thinking of that imitation he did of one of the 'Lucy' poems; we had better quote the texts:

A slumber did my spirit seal;
    I had no human fears:
She seemed a thing that could not feel
    The touch of earthly years.

No motion has she now, no force;
    She neither hears nor sees;
Rolled round in earth's diurnal course,
    With rocks, and stones, and trees.

The night is freezing fast,
    Tomorrow comes December;
        And winterfalls of old
Are with me from the past;
    And chiefly I remember
        How Dick would hate the cold.

Fall, winter, fall; for he,
    Prompt hand and headpiece clever,
        Has woven a winter robe,
And made of earth and sea
    His overcoat for ever,
        And wears the turning globe.

Housman has here followed Wordsworth fairly closely; the subject-matter is identical, except for the change of the dead person's gender, and the number of stanzas is the same, though the form is of course varied. Also, each poem brings in two figures; the dead person, and the 'I' through whom the situation is presented. On comparing them more closely, however, the first thing we become aware of is that Wordsworth has got much more into his eight lines than Housman has into his twelve; not only more emotional delicacy and intensity, but actually more in quantity. The 'I' of Housman's poem is static; his function is merely to say what has happened and to reminisce about past winters and how Dick hated the cold, in a way that reveals a rather mawkish feeling for the youth. Wordsworth's 'I', on the other hand, is as much the subject of the poem as the dead girl; whether we take the first stanza as self-criticism ('I was too complacent, because I was happy in my love for her; I did not think she could even age, and now she has gone and *died*'), or as a simple statement of a fact ('This is how so great a love makes you feel'), we are inescapably aware of the 'I' as an acting, feeling identity. Further, since so short a poem needs a certain antithetical balance of structure to give it the required density, we notice that this counterpart between his previous 'slumber' and *her* present insensibility to motion and force, gives the effect of balancing the two stanzas against one another. Wordsworth also manages to communicate, not precisely but unmistakably, that it is *because* of his lack of awareness that Lucy's death is so great a tragedy; if he had only been more alive to a natural process such as the passage of years, he would have valued his time with Lucy differently, and her pantheistic merging with the earth would not have seemed a privation, but merely a logical conclusion. The poem nowhere actually says this, but it is my experience (with students, etc.) that most readers pick up some such impression.

If we turn to the Housman immediately afterwards, the weaknesses of the lesser poet are thrown into startling relief. The whimsey of the diction ('headpiece', 'overcoat', in the same poem as 'robe', etc.) by comparison with the truthful simplicity of Wordsworth's; the silly suggestion that it was 'clever' of Dick to get into the earth to keep warm, by comparison with the tragic dignity of Wordsworth's pantheism! Even the over-artful stanza form seems vulgar by comparison, as also does the fake pastoralism of naming the boy 'Dick', thus lining him up with all the other lads and chaps in Housman's poetry.

Housman alone, of all the poets I have been discussing, had a public that was solidly behind him throughout his writing life; he was uncritically accepted as a genius from the moment he published his first volume, and even today any disparagement of his work is certain to be greeted by a chorus of protests. I don't want

I

to draw any crude moral from the fact that the best of these poets was the one who had least support from the 'reading public', and the worst the one who had most; but the reflection should help to calm those who are inclined to panic about the smallness of the public for poetry.

(1955)

THE QUALITY OF ARNOLD BENNETT

He stands nearer Gustave Flaubert than any other English novelist. — Georges Lafourcade

You can only do one man's modest share in the education of the public. — Arnold Bennett

Tell Mr. Bennett he stinks. — Anonymous telephone message, 1911.

THE re-issue of a batch of Arnold Bennett's novels by Penguin Books is a reminder of his curious position: he is much admired, but not (if this doesn't sound very rude) much admired by the people whose admiration is worth having. Obviously Georges Lafourcade was very intelligent, and he admired Bennett sufficiently to publish a long book about him in 1939, but foreigners, for this sort of purpose, don't count; Mr. Walter Allen came out with an able summary in the *English Novelists* series nine years later, but his efforts curiously failed to provide Bennett with any sort of highbrow reputation; perhaps the feeling was that Mr. Allen, being a Midlander and a novelist, was *bound* to like Bennett, so the rest of us didn't need to wonder if we ought to be converted. Then, of course, Lawrence is fashionable now, and he and Bennett are such opposites that there is hardly room for them on the same planet. Lawrence's reference to Bennett in his letter to A. V. McLeod, October 6, 1912, shows that he was clearly aware of this incompatibility: 'I hate Bennett's resignation. Tragedy ought to be a great kick at misery.' Dr. F. R. Leavis, who besides being Lawrentian-in-chief has the great prestige of being one of the few English critics to make a successful attempt at the criticism of fiction, has either picked up this view of Bennett from Lawrence, or come to it independently — it doesn't matter which; so we find him saying in *The Great Tradition*,

> for all the generous sense of common humanity to be found in his best work, Bennett seems to me never to have been disturbed enough by life to come anywhere near greatness.

121

I think this is a pity. How disturbed one has to be before great-ness becomes possible, I don't know, but Bennett has always seemed to me an excellent novelist, not so inferior to Lawrence as the current fashion would have us think. At any rate, here are a few notes on him, grouped into sections so that readers who find the whole too lengthy can skip any of the sections and still make sense of what they do read. The first section deals with the general mass of Bennett's work, the second with *The Old Wives' Tale*, the third with *Clayhanger* and the books that are ancillary to it, and the fourth with *Riceyman Steps*. My main object is to try to engage the serious novel-reader's interest, leaving the final judgement to him, but I am afraid my enthusiasm will now and then bounce me into a 'value-judgement'.

I

'Of pot-boilers let none speak. Jove hangs them on necks that could soar above his height, but for their accursed weight.' Bennett probably prided himself on the aptness of the quotation — it is from Meredith — yet the truth of the matter was, as re-gards his own case, exactly the opposite. Without the constant practice, without the habit of using the same material over and over again until finally he mastered it and gave it imaginative life, Bennett would never have produced his major work. This gives his mass of bread-and-butter novels a certain interest; they will never again be read by readers whose motive is entirely literary, and yet it is possible to draw from them some useful data about his methods of work and his preoccupations generally. In *The Author's Craft* (1914) he tends to talk as if there were only one kind of author and one kind of craft, and the outline he gives there of 'the author's' attitude is a fair description of his own: observa-tion first and foremost, but observation marshalled and directed to an end.

> The predominant interests of the observer [he says] will ultimately direct his observing activities to their own advantage. If excited by

the phenomena of organization — as I happen to be — he will see individuals in new groups that are the result of organization, and he will insist on the variations of type due to that grouping.

What are these groups into which individuals fall as the result of organization? Let us attempt a classification of the types that emerge most clearly from Bennett's novels.[1] To take the male characters first:

(i) Self-made men of the first generation (Darius Clayhanger, Mr. Povey, James Ollerenshaw). These are usually dominated by material considerations to an attempt that limits and controls their action in the plot. A variation of this type is the character whom the struggle for existence has warped and soured; Tellwright and Earlforward are misers, Critchlow a cynic.

(ii) The Card (Denry, Gerald Scales, Jos Curtenty). It will be seen, from a consideration of the characters I have bracketed here, that this type is only really at home in the lighter novels, and collapses into a profligate or villain when introduced into a serious book. Denry is a successful character *because* the writing is on the same level as a *Punch* cartoon: brilliant and wilfully incomplete.

(iii) The Sensitive Plant (Clayhanger, Lawrence Ridware, Willie Price, Richard Larch). This is the male type with whom Bennett had most sympathy, and the class includes some of his best portraits.

(iv) Neurotics and misfits. There is a surprisingly large number of these. Joe, Edgar and Geoffrey are nerve-shattered

---

[1] In the passage that follows it seemed necessary to identify only characters from the lesser-known novels; viz., James Ollerenshaw from *Helen With The High Hand*, Tellwright and Willie Price from *Anna of the Five Towns*, Jos Curtenty, a recurrent character in 'local-colour' in *Tales of the Five Towns*, Lawrence and Mark Ridware and Charles Fearns from *Whom God Hath Joined*, Edgar from *The Pretty Lady*, Geoffrey from *Lord Raingo*, Richard Larch from *A Man From the North*, Alan Frith-Walter from *Accident*, Johnnie Hulse from *The Glimpse*. Of the female characters mentioned, Annunciata Fearns is from *Whom God Hath Joined* and Christine from (indeed *is*) *The Pretty Lady*.

soldiers; Charles Fearns is a satyromaniac, Charlie Prohack a victim of social upheaval and war strain.

Finally, since Bennett's attitude to the arts seems to have been that they were, after all, simply the adjuncts of a high standard of living, we have two almost interchangeable types:

(v) The Man of the World with Artistic Tastes (G. J. Hoape, Matthew Peel-Swynnerton, Alan Frith-Walter, Johnnie Hulse). This seems to have been the type Bennett admired most; successful, leisured, sufficiently appreciative of the arts to enjoy them, and sufficiently Philistine to resist their strangling fascination.

Here is a specimen:

He himself was healthy and personable; young for his age. He had done excellently in the business, which, without positive enthusiasm for it, he liked. And he had interests wider than the business. He bought rare books, and a French picture occasionally. He had preferences among pianists, violinists, and orchestral conductors. He could go to a new play and despise it and yet enjoy bits of it. He understood food and wines and loved them. He could talk to his wife about her clothes with more knowledge and appreciation than she could talk to him about his.

We all recognize him at once: he is the tall, distinguished man, with a youthful bearing in strange contrast to his greying temples, who escorts fabulously dressed women through the advertisement pages in *Vogue*. The novelist's hero is the publicity man's dream. With only a slight shift of emphasis we reach

(vi) The Artist/Man of the World. This type is not compelled to earn his living, even at a business he likes ('without', of course, 'positive enthusiasm for it'). He has an income which allows him to devote himself to an Art. Sometimes he is really talented, sometimes not. Mark Ridware, for instance, never looked back after winning a national scholarship to the Royal College of Art, South Kensington; with the result that at the age of thirty-five 'His bearing had the touch of good-humoured arrogance which success so often gives . . . he . . . had reached the illustrated papers: no small achievement for a painter.' Whereas another national scholarship winner, Cyril Povey, remained a contented mediocrity.

The last two categories overlap so much that it is impossible to decide which of them ought to contain Loring, the British Museum æsthete who visits the Five Towns in Bennett's two best short stories. He is a good example of all the prevailing tendencies; a connoisseur in food, drink, tobacco, music, painting, first editions, newspapers, and smoking-room stories. This last detail is not unimportant; Bennett evidently believed that whenever two representatives of types (v) and (vi) met, their conversation sooner or later came round to 'life, in those aspects of it which cause men to laugh and women uneasily to wonder.' Even limericks can send up a man's prestige within these two groups.

It happened that I knew a number of the unprinted Rossetti limericks, precious things, not at all easy to get at. I detailed them to Mr. Brindley, and I do not exaggerate when I say that I impressed him. I recovered all the ground that I had lost upon cigarettes and newspapers.

Before leaving these two types we should note that they have a tendency to read Wordsworth in trains; but then Bennett evidently had what Professor Lafourcade rather disconcertingly calls 'a middle-class admiration for Wordsworth'.

The female characters are very easily arranged in groups. In any case it is obvious that most novelists, when drawing characters of the opposite sex, make a very sharp distinction between those who are sexually eligible and those who are not; I do not mean between good-looking and ugly, but between those biologically qualified for sexual relationships, and those who are *hors concours*.

If this sounds absurd, consider the vast superiority of the average female novelist's portraits of very old men, or children, over her portraits of men between twenty-one and sixty. Male novelists are less predictable, but it must be obvious that the same tendency is often present among them. In Bennett's work the older women (Mrs. Baines, Aunt Harriet, Mrs. Hamps, Mrs. Orgreave) are generally neutral, or, if they have a part in the plot, it is often a dead one; to be an obstruction against which the stream must push until it is dislodged. The hint, or echo, of crude scientific determinism in Bennett's mind may have been responsible for this: Mrs. Baines was 'at odds with the everlasting purpose' because it had 'made use of her and cast her aside'.

The younger women are generally either

(i) Shy, tender (Christine, Annunciata Fearns) or
(ii) Pert, wilful; a female counterpart to the Card type among the men (Ruth Earp, Helen Rathbone, Janet Orgreave).

In *The Old Wives' Tale* the two types are, of course, played off against each other in Constance and Sophia. The wide range of these two dominant types is illustrated by the fact that, of the two examples I have chosen to illustrate (i), one is a prostitute, the other a young girl of the most delicate sensibilities.

If this catalogue seems dull or unnecessary, I can only plead that it was Bennett himself who liked to 'see individuals in new groups that are the result of organization'; and that these groups are very important in surveying his work. For, on his view, so much depended on 'organization'; for instance, he takes it for granted that Samuel Povey, being a hard-working apprentice and later a respectable draper, will lead a decorous and moral life; just as he takes it for granted that his son, being a young man in easy circumstances with no responsibilities, will lead the life of pleasure and move in circles where women are discussed as if they were meat ('No more English for me'). The moral question does not arise; it is simply a question of environment and custom. He would probably have called this attitude 'scientific'.

Again, it may have been something to do with these half-grasped scientific doctrines that made him insist on the ruthlessness of children. Whatever the cause, he never introduces a child without some reference to its selfishness, sensuality, and contempt for the virtues. Mrs. Blackshaw's baby, a typical specimen, was

> convinced that the rest of the universe had been brought into existence solely for the convenience and pleasure of it — the baby . . . it had no god but its stomach. It never bothered its head about higher things. It was a bully and a coward, and it treated women as beings of a lower order than men. In short, it was that ideal creature, sung of the poets, from which we gradually sink and fall away as we grow older.[1]

This, of course, is nothing more than one of the commonest wiles of the trade: the facetious attribution of adult motives to the baby; but in his serious handling of the subject the same attitude is recognizable. Cyril Povey at the same stage

> had never spent a day without making experiments on this shifting universe in which he alone remained firm and stationary. The experiments were chiefly conducted out of idle amusement, but he was serious on the subject of food. Lately the behaviour of the universe in regard to his food had somewhat perplexed him, had indeed annoyed him. However, he was of a forgetful, happy disposition, and so long as the universe continued to fulfil its sole end as a machinery for the satisfaction, somehow, of his imperious desires, he was not inclined to remonstrate.

Both now and at a later stage, children are chiefly interesting to Bennett as a means of presenting and illustrating one of his favourite themes — misunderstanding. Parents behave insufferably to their children because they love them; children behave insufferably to their parents because they are inhabitants of a world totally different from, unguessed by, and inimical to the adult world. Bennett is at his finest when treating, with an admirable blend of irony and compassion, the inevitable conflict.

[1] 'Baby's Bath', in *The Grim Smile of the Five Towns*.

That superb children's party, when Cyril disgraces himself by snatching a slice of cake from one of his guests, is one of the minor peaks of English literature. Bennett's method is, here at least, entirely adequate to the situation; everything is accounted for, and the catastrophe is inevitable.

> His face at once changed from calm pride to a dreadful anxiety. His eyes bulged out. His tiny mouth grew and grew, like a mouth in a nightmare. He was no longer human; he was a cake-eating tiger being balked of his prey. Nobody noticed him. The officious fool of a woman persuaded Jennie to take the last slice of the cake, which was quite a thin slice.
>
> Then everyone simultaneously noticed Cyril, for he gave a yell. It was not the cry of a despairing soul who sees his beautiful iridescent dream shattered at his feet; it was the cry of the strong, masterful spirit, furious. He turned upon Jennie, sobbing, and snatched at her cake. Unaccustomed to such behaviour from hosts, and being besides a haughty, put-you-in-your-place beauty of the future, Jennie defended her cake. After all, it was not she who had taken two slices at once. Cyril hit her in the eye, and then crammed most of the slice of cake into his enormous mouth. He could not swallow it, nor even masticate it, for his throat was tight and rigid. So the cake projected from his red lips, and big tears watered it. The most awful mess you can conceive! Jennie wept loudly, and one or two others joined her in sympathy, but the rest went on eating tranquilly, unmoved by the horror which transfixed their elders.
>
> A host to snatch food from a guest! A host to strike a guest! A gentleman to strike a lady!

Here the same device as before, the application of adult standards to a child's behaviour, is used; but instead of being facetiously adopted by the author, it is satirically attributed to the grown-up witnesses. Everything is seen in a refreshingly right perspective. Cyril is an object of beauty to Bennett ('his tiny mouth'); he is also ruthlessly selfish ('a cake-eating tiger'); the woman who is helping to make the party a success is an 'officious fool'; and — finest touch of all — the utter isolation of the child-world from the adult-world is indicated by 'the rest went on eating tranquilly'. It is typical of Bennett's method that this superb episode should be a re-working of material that was already familiar to his readers; it was the patience of the competent journeyman that put greatness finally within his grasp.

II

There is no doubt that the theme of *The Old Wives' Tale* was alive in Bennett's mind before the story itself was planned. *Leonora* was at once recognized as an essay in this direction when it appeared in 1903; Marcel Schwob remarked that Bennett had 'got hold of the greatest of all themes — the agony of the older generation in watching the rise of the younger'.

The precise facts as to how this preoccupation took shape into a novel are common property. There are two sources for Bennett's account, of which the better known, his own preface to the later editions of the book, does not need to be quoted. The other is the Journal entry for November 18, 1903. This, as the reader is unlikely to have it by him, I quote in full.

Last night, when I went into the Duval for dinner, a middle-aged woman, inordinately stout and with pendant cheeks, had taken the seat opposite to my prescriptive seat. I hesitated, as there were plenty of empty places, but my waitress requested me to take my usual chair. I did so, and immediately thought: 'With *that* thing opposite to me my dinner will be spoilt!' But the woman was evidently also cross at my filling up her table, and she went away, picking up all her belongings, to another part of the restaurant, breathing hard. Then she abandoned her second choice for a third one. My waitress was scornful and angry at this desertion, but laughing also. Soon all the waitresses were privately laughing at the goings-on of the fat woman, who was being served by the most beautiful waitress I have ever seen at any Duval. The fat woman was clearly a crotchet, a 'maniaque', a woman who lived much alone. Her cloak (she displayed on taking it off a simply awful light puce flannel dress) and her parcels were continually the object of her attention and she was always arguing with her waitress. And the whole restaurant secretly made a butt of her. She was repulsive; no one could like her or sympathize with her. But I thought — she has been young and slim once. And I immediately thought of a long 10 or 15 thousand words short story. 'The History of Two Old Women'. I gave this woman a sister, fat as herself. And the first chapter would be in a restaurant (both sisters) something like tonight — and written rather cruelly. Then I would go back to the infancy of these two, and sketch it all. One should have lived ordinarily, married prosaically and become a widow. The other should have become a whore and all that; 'guilty splendour'. Both are overtaken by fat. And they live together again in old age, not too rich, a nuisance to themselves and to others. Neither has any imagination.

It will be seen that the published account is rather more tidy than what actually happened; the contrast between the two waitresses, the fat and faded one who served Bennett, and the beautiful one who caught his eye, is written up into something more striking than the Journal account warrants. The fat waitress, incidentally, was authentic enough; he continued to watch her and noted on November 19 that her looks were deceptive; 'fat, fifty, and apparently the image of shrewd content', she was 'really a *névrosée*, given to crises and sudden violent feelings of an irrational nature'. There is another slight discrepancy between the two accounts, in that the Preface describes the book as having been finished by the end of July 1908, while the Journal gives August 30 as the date; this may be mere carelessness.

One of the interesting points that arises from Bennett's account of the book's genesis, whichever version we consult, is the extent to which his fundamental honesty took command and forced him to tone down the obvious contrasts involved in his original idea; and also how his instinctive sympathy with humanity compelled him to produce in the end a book written in a manner the reverse of 'cruelly'. Sophia and Constance are not crudely opposite in temperament; they are simply different enough to be launched on different paths, which is not at all the same thing; nor are they ridiculous. As a matter of fact, however, Bennett did not sacrifice his original vision of the ridiculous and almost contemptible middle-aged woman. She is present clearly enough:

Her face, especially as damaged by tears, could not support the ordeal of inspection; it was horrible; not a picture, but a palette; or like the coloured design of a pavement artist after a heavy shower. Her great, relaxed eyelids alone would have rendered any face absurd; and there were monstrous details far worse than the eyelids. Then she was amazingly fat: flesh seemed to be escaping at all ends from a corset strained to the utmost limit. And above her boots — she was still wearing dainty, high-heeled, tightly laced boots — the calves bulged suddenly out.

As a woman of between forty and fifty, the obese sepulchre of a dead vulgar beauty, she had no right to passions and tears and homage, or even the means of life; she had no right to expose herself picturesquely beneath a crimson glow in all the panoply of ribboned garters and lacy seductiveness. It was silly; it was disgraceful. She ought to have known that only youth and slimness have the right to appeal to the feelings by indecent abandonments.

'The obese sepulchre of a dead vulgar beauty' — one has only to imagine the phrase applied to Constance or Sophia to realize the distance Bennett travelled in working out the novel. Yet they, by the end, are each the sepulchre of a beauty; and Constance, at any rate, is obese; the word is actually used of her. Nevertheless, the fat woman in the Duval did get into Bennett's story after all; and this fact redeems, for me at least, the not quite convincing character of Madame Foucault.

Just how hard and concentrated was the work of composing, of engineering, *The Old Wives' Tale*, we have plenty of striking evidence. Take, for instance, the much discussed point of chronology. It was not Bennett's way to set down precise dates as part of the narrative, but Maggie's written notice (Book II, cap. I) is dated June 10, 1867; this gives us the ages of Sophia and Constance, and by collecting the hints it is possible to give a date to every occurrence: death of John Baines, 1864; elopement of Sophia, 1865; marriage of Constance and Samuel, 1867; death of Mrs. Maddack, 1867; birth of Cyril Povey, 1874; death of Mrs.

Baines, 1875; and so forth. Constance's letter (Book IV, cap. I) enables us to check our calculations and provides a few missing links.

For the French sources, literary and historical, the world is largely in the debt of the late Professor Lafourcade's 'The Sources of the *Old Wives' Tale*' (in his *Arnold Bennett*, 1939). Not only did he discover the precise source of the account of Rivain's execution, in the articles by Georges de Labruyère in the *Matin* (August 22–27, 1907), but he showed that Bennett, while chiefly drawing on the account of the execution of one Eyrand (August 24, 26), borrowed the motive for Rivain's crime (the murder of a celebrated courtesan) from another case described in the same series. Lafourcade has also gone behind Bennett's bald statement of his sources for the Siege of Paris, and has shown in fascinating detail how many of the small touches of incident and description which give life to his narrative were carefully selected from the pages of Sarcey's *Le Siège de Paris* (1871). To say that his research had a direct bearing on criticism would be an under-statement; it is clear enough that there must be documentary evidence for the facts and figures about such matters as the price Sophia has to pay for black market food, but it is staggering to learn that the description of Chirac's ascent in the balloon is reproduced almost verbatim from Sarcey.

> The light of the railway engines [says Lafourcade], the colour of the taffetas, the presence of the Directeur des postes, the sailor, the mysterious figure wrapped in furs ('dont le nom est un mystère' — it probably *was* Chirac!), the pigeons, the forgotten victuals, the message from the governor, the perilous departure — all has been taken bodily from Sarcey.

Even the restaurant proprietor's joke about the dog's bone, even Sophia's exposure to the charge of signalling to the enemy as she carries her candle up and down stairs at night, have their origin in Sarcey. It is the modesty, the quiet skill, of Bennett's selection from facts, that is the mark of the master. He passed over the more lurid and flamboyant to seize, unerringly, on the small and telling. This tendency was no doubt strengthened by his conversation with the Leberts, from whom he rented the villa in which the book was written. They had been through the siege, but, he noted,

> they seemed only to attach importance to the siege because I did. Like inhabi-
> tants of picturesque town or curious village. [Italics his.] It seems to have
> left no particular mark on their minds. They thought more of an
> accident just before, and [of the fact that] they had a lot of potatoes.
> They had 3 children (went to school as usual). At first meal 125
> grammes each per day (but only 30 grammes later).

This seems to have been one of Bennett's main objects all through the book; to illustrate the faintness and remoteness of the impression made by great public upheavals on the individual life. It is not until potatoes become dearer that the war matters.

'Trade's bad', says John Baines, and Sophia

> was, in fact, aware of the badness of trade, caused by a vague war in the
> United States. The words 'North' and 'South' had a habit of re-
> curring in the conversation of adult persons. That was all she knew,
> though people were starving in the Five Towns, as they were
> starving in Manchester.

Again and again the distance of history-book events from personal life is stressed.

> As the two women strolled along, content with their industry and
> their resolves, they came to a National Guard, who, perched on a
> ladder, was chipping away the 'N' from the official sign of a court
> tradesman. It was in this way that Madame Foucault and Sophia
> learnt of the establishment of a republic.

It is this spirit that informs the fine paragraph in which Bennett muses over the death of John Baines.

> Mr. Critchlow and the widow gazed, helplessly waiting, at the
> pitiable corpse, of which the salient part was the white beard. They
> knew not that they were gazing at a vanished era. John Baines had
> belonged to the past, to an age when men really did think of their
> souls, when orators by phrases could move crowds to fury or to pity,

when no one had learnt to hurry, when Demos was only turning in his sleep, when the sole beauty of life resided in its inflexible and slow dignity, when hell really had no bottom, and a gilt-clasped Bible really was the secret of England's greatness. Mid-Victorian England lay on that mahogany bed. Ideals had passed away with John Baines. It is thus that ideals die; not in the conventional pageantry of honoured death, but ignobly, when one's back is turned —

There is an understanding of human history in that paragraph which radiates through the entire book.

This same patient restraint, which governed his selection of facts, is alive in the texture of Bennett's narrative. To analyse its workings in every particular would probably be more than the reader would stand for; but we might glance at the method of the opening chapters.

In almost every way, the first book of *The Old Wives' Tale* is the finest hundred pages Bennett ever wrote. This is fortunate, because the first book is strategically vital. Not only is the more important of the book's two settings established there, but almost every major character is introduced. Only Chirac, waiting in Paris, and Cyril, waiting to be born, were still ahead when Bennett sent Mrs. Baines to her living entombment at Axe. The first book deserves more than ordinary study.

The first thing one notices is the extraordinarily subtle use of anticipation. After the episode of the laudanum, when Sophia has run away to laugh in private, Constance stays with Mr. Povey. 'This seclusion of Constance and Mr. Povey was really very strange' — too slight, so far, even to be called a hint of what is ahead. The next pointer, in cap. iv, is: 'These two practical, duteous, common-sense young and youngish persons had been so absorbed in their efforts for the welfare of the shop that they had positively not only forgotten the time, but had also failed to notice the band.' That they were also engrossed in each other is almost imperceptibly conveyed, and underlined by the next sentence: 'But if Constance had had her wits about her she would at least have pretended that she had heard it.' By now the reader's suspicions are fully aroused, and he suddenly realizes that the shocking, unprecedented display of self-will by Constance — when she invaded Sophia's work-box to rescue Mr. Povey's tooth — was another sign of the state of her emotions. The joke had gone far enough: Mr. Povey's tooth was not to be kept as a comic souvenir. Everything is falling into place, and a few pages later the matter is settled. 'Who would have supposed that the gentle-eyed Constance, pattern of daughters, was risking her eternal welfare by smiling at the tailed one who, concealing his tail, had assumed the image of Mr. Povey?' (He, by the way, was thinking of the tickets they had been making.)

Again, the most alert of readers is unlikely to attach any importance to the fact that Mrs. Daniel Povey has a shocking hole in her curtains, and in a room overlooking the Square at that: but these things seep into the mind. A living care over detail is evident on every page. During Sophia's first interview with her father, Bennett quietly inserts, with no comment, two sentences that contain the explanation of his subsequent death.

Presently his sallow face and long white beard began to slip down the steep slant of the pillows, and a troubled look came into his left eye. Sophia rose and, putting her hands under his armpits, lifted him higher in the bed.

No comment — but that is how John Baines died. And not until it is too late does Bennett add explicitly, 'For five thousand nights she (Mrs. Baines) had wakened infallibly every time he stirred, and rearranged him by the flicker of a little oil lamp'. The handling of Gerald Scales is marked throughout by this triumphant subtlety of detail. We are led to identify ourselves so largely with Sophia that on a first reading, if we do not know the story, it is natural to see him as a knight errant; but the tiny drops of poison glitter so clearly that on a second reading we wonder how we could have missed them. Gerald's is a destructive role; every time he appears in this first book he breaks something, even if it is only

K

the decorum of the Baines parlour by using the word 'bitch', or Mrs. Baines's pride in her pastry. And Bennett does not forget to add, when John Baines is dead, the coolly significant words, 'The real murderer was having his dinner in the commercial room up at the Tiger, opposite the Town Hall'.

This patient precision is the main feature of Bennett's method in *The Old Wives' Tale*, just as its deep, half-articulate pity for humanity caught in the trap of Time is the main effect he is out to engineer. To say that this is obvious, to point out that no reader ever missed the point, is not to condemn Bennett for his triteness but to praise him for his success. His melancholy was not the re-action of the man who is 'disturbed' by life, but of one who was, if anything, frozen by it into a semi-paralytic suffering, of which the obverse is his frequently jarring jauntiness. But the irritating cocksure note is never permitted to enter this or any other of his major novels. What we get instead is a manly, uncomplaining melancholy, equally remote from peevishness or panic. It is use-less to try to show this by quotation, since Bennett's art is slow and cumulative; nevertheless, if I were asked to choose, from the pages of the work itself, phrases which contain the gist of its 'message', point, hub, centre, or whatever term is most in fashion, I should point to two. One is 'the vast inherent melancholy of the universe' (Book II, cap. 2, iii), and the other, 'the earth's fashion of renewing itself' (Book IV, cap. 2, i). In these two phrases, if we will weigh and examine them, is to be found the root of the matter. And along with his melancholy goes its proper accom-paniment, a gentle and dispassionate irony. This irony is present everywhere as a subsidiary colour. It is partly in the incidents: Constance does not go directly to Knype station to meet her sister, but deviously, so that it will not seem to observers that she is too excited; Mrs. Baines walks to the top of the Square to have a view of the new signboard, and returning, says nothing. And it is partly in the phrasing. 'She had caught smallpox and died of it,' Bennett remarks of Sophia's charwoman, 'thus losing a good situation'. When Spot is being forcibly washed, 'His eyes continually peeped forth between corners of the agitated towel, and they were full of inquietude and shame.'

Let me leave *The Old Wives' Tale* with a quotation in which, so it seems to me, the pathos and the irony achieve a perfect union. It is after the death of John Baines.

> . . . on the morning of the funeral Aunt Harriet had the satisfaction of beholding her younger sister the centre of a tremendous cocoon of crape, whose slightest pleat was perfect. Aunt Harriet seemed to welcome her then, like a veteran, formally into the august army of relicts.

Will not this suffice? Or must we still regret that he failed to launch 'a great kick at misery'?

III

Critics are fairly strongly agreed that Bennett's attempt at a trilogy was a failure; there is a disastrous slipping on to an altogether lower plane in the second book, and the third is merely a perfunctory rounding-off which would not really save the situation even if it were a success in itself, which it is not. Nevertheless there is something to be gained from a discussion of the extent to which the books do fit together. *Clayhanger* is not improved by the addition of *Hilda Lessways* and *These Twain*, but even so the subsequent volumes are worth reading, and most of their readability is owing to the interest already aroused in the magnificent opening study. As for *The Lion's Share*, it is too late to try to defend that. It adds nothing at all.

I suppose most of Bennett's readers have gone through *Hilda Lessways*, even if their interest flagged before reading *These Twain*, because there are some important episodes in *Clayhanger* that are deliberately meant to be unintelligible without an account of Hilda's actions and motives. This kind of book must be hard to write, and there was not much to guide him; the only masterpiece of this kind in previous English fiction is Hogg's *Confessions of a Justified Sinner*, which he does not seem to have known; and which anyway was a special case, having an occult theme. The trouble in *Hilda Lessways* is that Bennett fails, almost entirely, to give us any understanding of Hilda's character even when he devotes a whole book to her. A few details of plot are cleared up — we learn who George Cannon was, and why she married him, and why she had to disappoint Edwin when he was waiting to show her over the printing works — but the light shed on the source and essence of her behaviour is far too dim. The key to her character, we are given to understand, lies in the intensity with which she savours life; she is always realizing this or that 'in a flash', odd sensations about the miracle of life keep coming over her, and so forth, but the reader can never do more than watch it happening from the outside. The words 'romantic' and 'romance', always favourites with Bennett, are cruelly overworked; so much so as to suggest that his failure to convince is intimately connected with a purely stylistic bankruptcy. After Hilda's first visit to George Cannon, 'The whole town, the whole future, seemed to be drenched now in romance'. When she first saw a specimen of Pitman's shorthand, 'In their mysterious strokes and curves and dots she saw romance'. Then there is 'the strange, romantic piquancy' of her 'brief vision' of Edwin: 'all her being vibrated to the mysterious and beautiful romance of existence'. When her mother's house and furniture were sold, she was affected by the thought that so elaborate and decisive an undertaking had gone forward merely at her command: 'How mysteriously romantic,' Bennett comments. Cannon's demeanour 'seemed . . . to give romance to the perfectly unromantic business of lodging and catering'. Her first sight of Brighton 'made promises to her romantic sense'. The fact that a joint responsibility for Sarah Gailey's welfare was forming a link between herself and Cannon 'seemed to her grandiose and romantic'. In the room where he proposed to her 'she saw glimpses, beautiful and compensatory, of the romantic quality of common life'. She had never been in that room before, and 'she regarded the fact as tremendously romantic'. Edwin's face, to her, 'was romantic, melancholy, wistful, enigmatic'. Examples could be multiplied for pages. Of course, too, she is continually vibrating, yearning and burning: the fact must be driven home that she is *intense*. At the sight of the ill-clad, thin figures of the strikers' children, 'Pain and joy ran together in her, burning exquisitely; and she had a glimpse, obscure, of the mystical beauty of the child's suffering'. The extent to which Bennett had lost his head is painfully evident from the fact that he blots out his usual clear, honest vision of human life and begins to talk nonsense (for nonsense, in a man of his beliefs and temperament, it is) about suffering having a 'mystical beauty'. 'Bliss' is another favourite word for Hilda's emotions. The first time she reminded George Cannon to drink his evening glass of milk, 'The fact that he had forgotten it and she had remembered it yet further increased her strange, mournful, ecstatic bliss'. And of Edwin: 'The idea that all his life had been embittered and shadowed by the caprice of an old man was beautiful to her in its sadness: she contemplated it with vague bliss'.

The fact is that Bennett is out of his depth. It is remarkable that a man so preoccupied with, and versed in, the method of fiction, should not have realized that repeated statement, by the author, of the nature of a character's emotions is no substitute for an imaginative presentation which will communicate these emotions. In his hack-work one is prepared for it (cf. *Mr. Prohack*, where the reiterated statement that Prohack loved his wife is made to do duty for an imaginative perception of his love, which alone would have given point to his mental conflict); but in a book designed to stand beside *Clayhanger* it is a bad disappointment.

There are, of course, other reasons for the inferiority of *Hilda Lessways*. In *Clayhanger* the love story had been only one strand of many, and is in fact subordinated to the main theme, that of growing up. Here the love story is weakened by being largely unsupported. True, Bennett meant to support it; just as in *Clayhanger* the action was seen as part of a provincial adolescence, so now it is meant to be seen as part of the development of a sensitive and poetic woman, a kind of Sophia Baines, but with more soul and less selfishness — or rather a different kind of self-absorption. But he simply had not sufficient weight of material. It is all too much of a *mélange* of things he had treated before: the lonely woman with her life running down, the intimate life of a household, the position of domestic servants, the strangeness of Brighton to a provincial — all had been dealt with to exhaustion; it is simply the popular novelist's method of writing the same book over and over again.

This is not to say that *Hilda Lessways* can be overlooked. It contains some of the finest pages Bennett ever wrote, and even seen as a whole it shows a sombre awareness of the depth and force of everyday incident worthy of the best traditions of the realistic novel. The description of Hilda's sensations during her nervous collapse, in which she imagines herself to have been transformed into the hideous epileptic whom she saw in the street, is on a level with the similar incident in the life of Sophia Baines; and for a crowning example there is the attempted suicide of Sarah Gailey.

> Hilda ran down the steps; at the bottom another row of lamps defined the shore, and now she could hear the tide lapping ceaselessly amid the supporting ironwork of the pier. She at once descried the figure of Sarah Gailey in the gloom. The woman was moving towards the faintly white edge of the sea. Hilda started to run after her, first across smooth asphalt, and then over some sails stretched out to dry; and then her feet sank at each step into descending ridges of loose shingle, and she nearly fell. At length she came to firm sand, and stood still.
>
> Sarah Gailey was now silhouetted against the pale shadows of foam that in ever-renewed curves divided the shore from the sea. After a time, she bent down, rose again, moved towards the water, and drew back. Hilda did not stir. She could not bring herself to approach the lonely figure. She felt that to go and accost Sarah Gailey would be indelicate and inexcusable. She felt as if she were

basely spying. She was completely at a loss, and knew not how to act. But presently she discerned that the white foam was circling round Sarah's feet, and that Sarah was standing careless in the midst of it. And at last, timid and shaking with agitation, she ventured nearer and nearer. And Sarah heard her on the sand, and looked behind.

'Miss Gailey!' she appealed in a trembling voice.

Sarah made no response of any kind, and Hilda reached the edge of the foam.

'Please, please don't stand there! You'll catch a dreadful cold, and you've got nothing on your shoulders either!'

'I want to make a hole in the water,' said Sarah miserably. 'I wanted to make a hole in the water!'

'Please do come back with me!' Hilda implored; but she spoke mechanically, as though saying something which she was bound to say, but which she did not feel.

I am not sure how this extract will strike readers who are not familiar with the whole novel; but in its context it is the climax of a very great study in human misery. The fact that Bennett could expend so much passion, and muster so skilfully the resources of his craft, in drawing the figure of Sarah Gailey is not to be explained simply as the professional wish to exploit a line which had proved profitable. On the contrary; it is a sign that the complex perceptions and emotions which prompted the earlier study were still unexhausted; it is like (in its immeasurably smaller but still valid way) the repetition, in *Cymbeline*, of the theme of *Othello*.

These Twain, which followed at a distance of nearly five years, is of little value except as a pendant to *Clayhanger*. The ostensible theme — marriage — is treated with a curious lack of conviction (five years later Bennett's own marriage collapsed, but this may be nothing to do with the matter). Edwin and Hilda occupied such obviously different planes of their creator's mind, the one seen from within, the other from without, that he was courting failure in the attempt to show their life together. Nevertheless there are a number of dramatically excellent moments, in which time-bombs planted in *Clayhanger* suddenly explode. One of these is the death of Auntie Hamps; others, more sharply defined, are incidents which reveal the consequences of the moral attitudes which formed Edwin's early environment. The way of life typified by Darius, Albert Benbow, and Auntie Hamps is shown in its effect on human relationships; this kind of work is extremely subtle, and Bennett was right to allow himself a fresh book to turn round in.

To take a striking example:

> Maggie had once said that she knew that Auntie Hamps made her servant eat dripping instead of butter. To give inferior food to a servant was to Maggie the unforgivable in parsimony (*Clayhanger*, cap. VII).

After hundreds of pages, and some thirty-five years, we reach the chapter in which Maggie, who has gone to live with Auntie Hamps, is directing the household while the old woman lies upstairs dying. The servant-girl comes in for her supper.

> 'Here's your bread,' said Maggie, indicating the two rounds of dry bread. 'I've left the dripping on the kitchen table for you.'

The shock is all the keener in that Bennett does not, for once, pause to underline. He says that Edwin was 'revolted' as he 'perceived in a flash what the life of Minnie was under the régime of Auntie Hamps'. But the more important point — that Maggie has become resigned to administering this régime, even to the details which had once struck her as 'the unforgivable in parsimony', is left to the reader to pick up.

Consider, again, the remarkably significant parallel between the tea-party in the early pages of *Clayhanger*, and the corresponding tea-party at the home of the Benbows in *These Twain*. In each, there is a mutely suffering child, oppressed by the severity of his elders and even more oppressed by their smug acts of 'kindness'. Edwin, at the first party, is feverishly anxious to seize some opportunity of announcing his decision to seek an independent career; Bert Benbow, at the second, is depressed because his birth-

day has been ruined by the elephantine unction of his parents'
celebration of it. And there is the clinching parallel: at each party
Auntie Hamps, choosing her moment for its effectiveness, leans
across and raps down half a sovereign on the boy's plate. The fact
of her presence — a member of the older generation at the first
party, still surviving and still authoritative at the second — gives
just the necessary point to the repetition. For the heart of the
matter is that the Bursley generations succeed one another un-
altered; still smug, still 'acting for the best', still stifling their
children's lives through lack of imagination. Here is Edwin:

After all, it was not a crime, it was no cause for shame to wish not
to be a printer. Yet he was ashamed! Absurd! He blamed himself.
But he also blamed his father. Now, however, in responding to his
auntie's remark [she has said, 'It does me good to think what a *help*
you'll be to your father in the business'], he could remedy all the past
by simply and boldly stating that he did not want to follow his father.
It would be unpleasant, of course, but the worst shock would be over
in a moment, like the drawing of a tooth. He had merely to utter
certain words. He must utter them. They were perfectly easy to say,
and they were also of the greatest urgency. 'I don't want to be a
printer.' He mumbled them over in his mind. 'I don't want to be a
printer.' What could it matter to his father whether he was a printer
or not? Seconds, minutes, seemed to pass. He knew that if he was so
inconceivably craven as to remain silent, his self-respect would never
recover from the blow.

And here is Bert Benbow:

Spectacles had been ordained for him by the oculist, and his parents
had had the hardihood to offer him his first pair for a birthday
present. They had so insisted on the beauty and originality of the
scheme that Bert himself had almost come to believe that to get a
pair of spectacles for a birthday present was a great thing in a boy's
life. He was now wearing the spectacles for the first time. On the
whole, gloom out-balanced pride in his demeanour, and Bert's
mysterious soul, which had flabbergasted his father for about a week,
peeped out sidelong occasionally through those spectacles in bitter
criticism of the institution of parents. . . . His presents, all useful

(save a bouquet of flowers from Rupert), were all useless to him. Thus the prim young Clara had been parentally guided to give him a comb. If all the combs in the world had been annihilated Bert would not have cared, — would indeed have rejoiced. And as to the spectacles, he would have preferred the prospect of total blindness in middle age to the compulsion of wearing them. Who can wonder that his father had not fathomed the mind of the strange creature?

This is the Bennett who matters, the Bennett for whose absence English fiction would be the poorer. But it cannot be denied that *These Twain*, taken on its own (and each panel of a trilogy should, obviously, be able to sustain criticism alone) does not succeed. Bennett's power of organization seems to have deserted him. The character of Tertius Ingpen, for instance, is meant to embody an important comment, or series of comments, on marriage; he is the unattached and unhampered bachelor whose life, contrasting with Edwin's, throws into relief the joys and exasperations of wedlock. But Ingpen is so loosely and casually linked with the story, his appearances are so haphazard, as to leave the impression of untidiness; an impression necessarily fatal to an art such as Bennett's. Even the final — and rather desperate — attempt to bully his material into a unified form, comes too late. Edwin, moodily pacing about the streets at night while he screws himself up to the point of deciding whether or not to break up his marriage, comes to that same canal bridge on which, scores of chapters earlier, he had stood on his way home from school. He recalls that 'as a boy he could not sit on the parapet unless he vaulted up to it. He thought he must have been ridiculously small and boyish.' A good touch, but too late. The house has collapsed, and it is of no use to exhibit the foundations, however deeply they were dug.

Nevertheless, when the painful duty of assessing the degree of failure of the rest of the trilogy has been performed, the one great volume, unshaken, valid, and almost self-sufficient, remains. On January 5, 1910, at a quarter to ten in the morning, Bennett sat down and began the writing of *Clayhanger*.

I felt less nervous and self-conscious than usual in beginning a book. And never before have I made one-quarter so many preliminary notes and investigations.

This was true. He had consulted Shaw's *North Staffordshire Potteries*, the 'Social and Industrial' section of the Victoria History,[1] and an anonymous book by 'An Old Potter' called *When I was a Child*. He had even gone to the length of making a list of the chief 'social, political and artistic events' between 1872 and 1882; and to round off his researches he had paid a visit to the Potteries in December 1909 during which he spent a good many hours in the company of Joseph Dawson, a shopkeeper and the Registrar of Burslem. On December 8, after a morning during which he 'made real progress in getting information from Dawson', he went to the local theatre; the show included some clog-dancing, which impressed him so much that he immediately (and characteristically) envisaged a short article about it for the *Nation*. (All Bennett's inspirations came to him originally in the form of ideas for short stories or articles, and ended by being digested into his larger schemes.) Altogether, the last few weeks before he began to write the novel were spent in polishing and enlarging his knowledge of its subject matter. He even went for a walk along the route that Edwin would take on returning from his last day at school. This novel was to be (*un*) *des plus historiques de ce temps-ci* with a vengeance.

He had every right, then, to feel 'less self-conscious and nervous than usual'. With *The Old Wives' Tale* behind him, and his theme

[1] Thus the Journal: it is actually 'Social and Economic' (pp. 275–319 in ed. of 1908). It is no surprise to find Bennett deliberately omitting the more horrific details he read there, *e.g.* that 'Most of the workhouses suffered from inadequate classification of inmates, so that one might find able-bodied men, women and children, all herded together in a horrible community'. On the other hand he has picked and chosen his material delicately; there is not much evidence that Darius would have gone to work as an apprentice at the age of six, for in the pottery trade the normal starting age was thirteen (p. 307). But his eye was no doubt caught by a sentence two pages earlier which actually refers to children apprenticed to the hardware trade in South Staffordshire: 'They began to work at the age of seven or eight, sometimes as early as six, and their hours of work were without limit save that ultimately set by human endurance'.

and setting entirely at his finger-tips, there was no reason why he should not set out deliberately to write the greatest regional novel in English literature. Moreover, he was aiming well within his known range. He had proved himself capable of dealing separately with all the themes and subjects which he now proposed to treat in combination — with the Five Towns, with adolescence, with illness and death, with Victorian commerce, with 'the great war between the old and young'.

It was merely a question of organization, and he had shown his strength in organization a score of times. As the book's preparation had been careful and leisurely, so its composition was regular and uninterrupted. Perhaps too regular, too quiet, for its author's peace of mind. 'I am trying to lift the whole thing up to a great height, but I feel sure that up to now it is nothing more than interesting in a nice quiet way,' he noted after working on it for sixteen days. On June 12, in a moment of surfeit after writing 2,400 words in twelve hours, he felt gently pessimistic. 'I really doubt whether as a whole, this book is good. It certainly isn't within ten miles of Dostoevsky.' This did not prevent his persevering, and on July 23 the task was done. 'I have just (3 p.m.) finished *Clayhanger* one week in advance of time.' Mental efficiency had triumphed.

Like *The Old Wives' Tale*, *Clayhanger* is in a sense a novel about time. The passage of time, 'the earth's fashion of renewing itself', becomes a poetic theme on its own. Technically this is done by the slow accumulation of minute changes and adjustments, with every now and then a shock of surprise as we realize that some great change has become inevitable and has duly happened. Imaginatively it is done by Bennett's usual insistence on the wonder that lies under the surface of any normal life. Mr. Shushions's life is grasped at the tail end, and we are made to feel, without much retrospect, the immense distance of years that lies behind him: Darius Clayhanger enters the book middle-aged, and grows old and dies in its pages, but in his case there is a determinedly full retrospect, and the 'little boy from the Bastille' refrain, to emphasize the hugeness of this unremarkable existence; Edwin's thirty-five years seem, as in true realism they were bound to, like a century. Not only in the book's construction, but in countless scattered remarks, the great length of a few years, to those who have to live them, is emphasized. 'The Sunday' was given that nickname by his schoolfellows, but no one knew why. 'Its origin was lost in the prehistoric ages of his childhood.' Only a man who understood an important fact about childhood — its appalling length — could have written that sentence.

Besides the time theme, or rather linked to it, is the book's 'second subject': growing up. Edwin, whose character is such that he shrinks from any kind of violence or conflict, is driven by impulses at the centre of his being to revolt from his environment, and his love for Hilda is not so much a third subject as a subdivision of the second. She represents the opposite of everything he is seeking to escape. In the fight for his own soul, his father is the arch-enemy, Clara a thorn in his flesh, and Mrs. Hamps a dead weight, not actively hostile, but uncertain, likely at any moment of tension to crash down on the other side of the scale and out-balance his will with hers.

The economy with which the characters are apportioned to the theme is typical of Bennett's good work. As in *The Old Wives' Tale*, one parent is sufficient (Edwin's mother, long dead, is scarcely mentioned) though an outside figure with something of a parental status is useful (Mr. Critchlow — Auntie Hamps). Every character is used to throw important light on the figure of Edwin, while at the same time each adds his mite of 'romance' to the slow unfolding of the years. The minor characters are chiefly useful as embodiments of the Bursley spirit from which Edwin struggles to free himself; some are contemptible, but not hateful (Albert Ben-bow), others sympathetic (Big James). The Orgreave family is of great importance, not only for the plot — a machinery for intro-ducing Hilda into Edwin's world — but because they typify the life to which Edwin aspires and gradually ascends. It is symbolic of the faint but haunting note of failure, which sounds repeatedly through the book, that the Orgreaves should later (in *These Twain*) succumb to financial ruin, and that Janet Orgreave should finally be shown as an unwanted, brightly pathetic spinster.

When all is said, the finest quality of *Clayhanger* is the finest quality of all Bennett's work: his understanding. He does not take sides. If he happens to prefer Edwin to Darius, it is not because he does not understand Darius. He understands them both, just as each of them misunderstands the other. As Mr. Pritchett has neatly put it, 'Each one bumps awkwardly along in the wonder of his own nature'.

Everything in *Clayhanger* is so perfectly understood, so entirely assimilated by the novelist's imagination, that it must nearly be impossible to read it without gaining in wisdom. But it is a brown, flat, autumnal wisdom that he gives us. Everything, everyone, is on a small scale. Edwin's education was futile; Methodism is crude and somehow sinister; Maggie lives and dies for no reason in particular; Albert and Clara are coarsely stupid; the Five Towns are dull and heavy, Brighton is vulgar. Lives fizzle out, and no one has much idea of what it all means. Human nature is represented throughout as something rather grey and wizened. For instance:

> When they entered the shining mahogany interior of the richest Bank in the Five Towns, hushed save for a discreet shovelling of coins, Edwin waited for his father to speak, and Darius said not a word, but stood glumly quiescent, like a victim in a halter. The little wiry dancing cashier looked; every clerk in the place looked; from behind the third counter, in the far recesses of the Bank, clerks looked over their ledgers; and they all looked in the same annoying way, as at a victim in a halter; in their glance was all the pitiful gloating baseness of human nature, mingled with a little of its compassion.

It is this kind of passage that would naturally occur to Bennett's opponents as illustration of his negative, resigned attitude. And yet a mere reading of it, particularly in its context, reveals a force of counter-assertion, a vehemence of suppressed but communicated protest, that turns the apparent negation into something affirmative. People talk as if Bennett were *glad* about the pitiful gloating baseness of human nature, yet the whole tendency of his work is to show how it is inextricably blended with compassion.

IV

There remains only *Riceyman Steps* (1923), the novel with which Bennett confounded the contemporary opinion that he was played out. In a sense, opinion was right; he was tired, worried, and disillusioned, and he succeeded by capitalizing these very elements. His art had never been exuberant, and now he marshalled all the resources of his experience to express in art — with all 'the force and beauty of its process' — his own incapacity to see beyond a world of suffering and misunderstanding. George Moore's remark, that it was 'the only really objective novel ever written', may be taken as a recognition of its extreme honesty and plainness; if he meant that Bennett had been more than usually successful in keeping himself out of the way, one cannot agree.

Riceyman Steps must be the most *stationary* novel in English. Previously Bennett had excelled in showing the enormously slow and crowded passage of time; here, time stops altogether. All the characters are fully developed when the book begins, and though they perform actions they are not really acting, in any deep sense, at all: they are pacing about inside the cage that was built and locked round them before the first sentence was written. The only element of suspense, on a first reading, lies in one's anxiety to know by what means Elsie will finally escape from the cage. Escape she will, for she alone of the three principal characters has the atmosphere of life about her. Violet, from the first, is a victim; ripe for sacrifice from the moment she appears, by reason of her independent means, her sensible attractiveness, and her bright common-sense brand of stinginess, she is twisted and twisted in the web until it hides her struggles.

That is the point about Mr. Earlforward: he is a spider, but a bland and gentle one. He does not spin webs with the intention of laying them as traps for flies. He spins them because he cannot help it; the sticky grey thread exudes from him automatically, and, as he goes about what for him is normal life, his fellow creatures are imprisoned and left to starve. That is why Bennett insists throughout the book not only on his blandness, but on his easy indifference, his faculty of letting things slide. The positive passion, the mania, which is the centre of the miserly character, is of course present; but it is hidden in a soft centre of indifference, and when it appears it is always directed most fiercely at himself rather than at others. He starves himself; he endures the agony of strain in his lame leg rather than ride in a taxi; he refuses to have the doctor or to be taken to hospital. It is admirably in keeping with this conception of his character that he should have *inherited* the bookshop, with all its paraphernalia of casual acquisitiveness, and not built it up himself. This, one gathers, fostered his reluctance to part with money, rather than any passion for making it. He buys and sells cheaply; he does not object to a little rain falling on the cheap books outside; rather than give a ten-shilling note to charity, he prefers to give a book whose potential value is probably as many pounds. All this is logical, even simple, but fiction had hitherto neglected the spider in its misers and concentrated on the tiger.

But to return to the first point. This is not a story; it is what the Elizabethans would have called an anatomy. There are three *active* characters: Elsie, Mr. Earlforward, and Dr. Raste; and two *passive* characters, Violet and Joe. These two are passive in that their function is to have things done to them by the active characters, thus enabling the active characters to be better understood. It does not depend on frequency of appearance. Violet, for all her central position in the book, and for all her surges of resolute

action, is a passive character, and Raste, whose part in the plot is
slight, is active, for he influences both Elsie and the miser. He is
the real opponent of Earlforward when it comes to a struggle
over the question of going into hospital, and he provides the
destination, offstage, to which Elsie moves when the finishing
touch is given to the portrait by the logical and necessary double
death; a destination which we never see, but which emanates
waves of its own atmosphere into the miser's house, waves which
have almost the importance of a character in the story. The
doctor's house represents normality; since there is a child and a
pet animal there, it also represents life as opposed to the atmosphere of death in the bookshop; since it is where Joe is employed,
it also represents salvation for Elsie.

So many people have commented on the narrowness of *Riceyman Steps* that it is worth remarking, briefly, on the extreme importance of the double plot in the book. The value of double plots
in the drama is nowadays fairly well realized, owing no doubt to
Mr. Empson's classic essay, but there is room for more recognition of its usefulness to the novelist. Elsie, the one *living* character
at the centre of the plot, is occupied during most of the book in
two ways; her body is working for the Earlforwards, and her soul
is waiting for the return of Joe; in other words, she is the spectator
of death, and she is waiting for the recommencement of life. The
union of death (Mr. and Mrs. Earlforward) is in contrast to, and
the enemy of, the union of life (Joe and Elsie). In terms of plot,
they are related by the fact that Joe's homicidal outbreak, which
was the cause of his decision to absent himself for a year, arose
from the fact that Elsie was made to work overtime for Violet,
and could not spend the evening with him on his birthday; and
later by the simultaneous presence of Joe and Earlforward in the
house, both ill and both tended by Elsie. The handling of these
two plots is, in my opinion, Bennett's finest technical achievement. The Joe–Elsie plot reaches a climax of tension in Book IV,
cap. V, when Elsie spends the last hour of the year in an agony

L

of half-expectant anxiety, and Joe does not come. Then the Earlforward plot moves strongly into the foreground; Nemesis over-
takes the doomed couple, and the reader forgets completely about
Joe because Elsie herself forgets. Violet, dying, is carried off to
hospital, Earlforward himself is dying, and Elsie is in command.
She sends Mrs. Perkins's boy on an errand to the hospital; and just
as he is about to depart —

> 'Your Joe's been asking for you to-night,' he said suddenly.
> 'My Joe!' She stood still, then leaned against the railings.

Riceyman Steps is not the best novel Bennett wrote, but it is the
most brilliant. A man of fifty-six, whose strength had previously
lain in the honest, leisurely chronicling of normal life, suddenly
forsook his usual line and produced, not a novel at all, but a disguised poem; for a poem it is, with its surges of half-revealed
emotion conveyed by imagery, with its crests and troughs of
rhythm. Knowing Bennett, one looks back for a precursor among
his early failures and half-successes; lighting, inevitably, on *Anna
of the Five Towns*. That fierceness, that intensity and concentration,
would have marked the earlier novel had it succeeded. But Bennett had not yet learnt the secret of such writing. It is characteristic
of him that he laboured in pursuit of that secret for twenty-one
years; and no less characteristic that finally, unmistakably, he
found it out.

V

If Bennett is to be placed in literary history, I should say that
he came at the end of that branch of English fiction which was
begun by Defoe. The two so obviously counterbalance each
other; the one inaugurating that particular kind of precision, the
other bringing it to its highest point (and at the same time flogging
it to death). Both were journalists who disciplined themselves into
novelists by long and strenuous apprenticeship; both were pro-
ducts of the mercantile middle class — that class which was just

reaching its full stature in Defoe's day, and just beginning to dwindle into something smaller and shabbier in Bennett's. And their minds are extraordinarily similar; brisk, entirely mundane, tinged with Philistinism, strong rather than fine. They have the same sense of humour, chiefly manifest in a kind of dry, deflating irony: compare 'She had caught smallpox and died of it, thus losing a good situation' with

> My good gipsy mother, for some of her worthy actions no doubt, happened in process of time to be hanged: and as this fell out something too soon for me to be perfected in the strolling trade, the parish where I was left . . . took care of me (*Captain Singleton*).

Bennett is richer, of course, but only (one feels) because he has two centuries more of European fiction to draw on. If Defoe had been able to read Flaubert and Dostoevsky, it is absurd to suppose that he would not have profited by them, at least to the extent of basing his stories on something more than the simple profit-and-loss attitude to life. Another parallel, of course, lies in the completeness with which nine-tenths of Defoe's output has withered away, leaving him represented by about four books.

There is, however, one important difference between the two. Defoe is fascinated by life, by the variety of things that can happen to a man; Bennett is numbed at the ultimate monotony of the pattern. In spite of what may happen on the surface, he seems to be thinking, human lives vary so little, so pitifully little. Even at his most light-hearted he seldom writes a page in which we cannot hear the distant clank of the chain, reminding us that, after all, these people are prisoners. Even *The Card*, one of the funniest books ever written, has its Widow Hullins. Look at her:

> The old woman sat at the fireplace, 'all bunched up,' as they say in the Five Towns. The only fire in the room, however, was in the short clay pipe which she smoked; Mrs. Hullins was one of the last old women in Bursley to smoke a cutty; and even then the pipe was considered coarse, and cigarettes were coming into fashion — though not in Chapel Alley. Mrs. Hullins smoked her pipe, and thought

about nothing in particular. Occasionally some vision of the past floated through her drowsy brain. She had lived in that residence for over forty years. She had brought up eleven children and two husbands there. She had coddled thirty-five grandchildren there, and given instruction to some half-dozen daughters-in-law. She had known midnights when she could scarcely move in that residence without disturbing somebody asleep. Now she was alone in it. She never left it, except to fetch water from the pump in the square. She had seen a lot of life, and she was tired.

It is a not particularly profound or far-reaching comment on life, but it seems to me to be valid; the kind of comment that can be properly made by the realistic novel. And is it so certain, after all, that Virginia Woolf's criticism has really disposed of that *genre* for ever? True, it must have been a Magna Carta when she first uttered it:

> Admitting the vagueness which afflicts all criticism of novels, let us hazard the opinion that for us at this moment the form of fiction most in vogue more often misses than secures the thing we seek. Whether we call it life or spirit, truth or reality, this, the essential thing, has moved off, or on, and refuses to be contained any longer in such ill-fitting vestments as we provide. Nevertheless, we go on perseveringly, conscientiously, constructing our two and thirty chapters after a design which more and more ceases to resemble the vision in our minds. So much of the enormous labour of providing the solidity, the likeness to life, of the story is not merely labour thrown away but labour misplaced to the extent of obscuring and blotting out the light of the conception. The writer seems constrained, not by his own free will but by some powerful and unscrupulous tyrant who has him in thrall, to provide a plot, to provide comedy, tragedy, love interest, and an air of probability embalming the whole so impeccable that if all his figures were to come to life they would find themselves dressed down to the last button of their coats in the fashion of the hour. The tyrant is obeyed; the novel is done to a turn. But sometimes, more and more often as time goes by, we suspect a momentary doubt, a spasm of rebellion, as the pages fill themselves in the customary way. Is life like this? Must novels be like this? (*Mr. Bennett and Mrs. Brown*, 1924.)

What this boils down to is a plea for a new convention, one that would involve a keener recognition that 'life is a luminous halo, a semi-transparent envelope surrounding us from the beginning of consciousness to the end'. And several new conventions have duly been tried out, and found to have their own limitations. *The Years* is an attempt in the same direction as *The Old Wives' Tale*, but can we honestly say that it is equally successful? In stressing the falsity of the accumulative realist method, Mrs. Woolf was not, one feels, allowing sufficient importance to the work done by the reader. The right kind of reader can extract a rich poetic experience from the heaviest and most matter-of-fact compilation, *so long as it is honest*; in fact it is easier to respond richly to this kind than to the over-lush imaginative novel that provides your poetry for you.

And, in any case, Bennett would have been the last to deny that conventions in fiction come and go. One of his essays, written in 1910 — it is to be found in *Books and Persons*, 1917 — is almost prophetic in this respect. He is discussing modernism in the arts generally, and though he takes little enough pleasure in it he admits that it sharpens and strengthens his instinct for quality. '. . . a regular contemplation of these pictures [*i.e.* those of Matisse and Vallotton] inspires a weariness of all other pictures that are not absolutely first rate.' Then follows a statement on his own art that seems to me of great importance.

I have permitted myself to suspect that supposing some writer were to come along and do in words what these men have done in paint, I might conceivably be disgusted with nearly the whole of modern fiction, and I might have to begin again. This awkward experience will in all probability not happen to me, but it might happen to a younger writer than me. At any rate, it is a fine thought. The average critic always calls me, both in praise and dispraise, 'photographic'; and I always rebut the epithet with disdain, because in the sense meant by the average critic I am not photographic. But supposing that in a deeper sense I were? Supposing a young writer turned up and forced me, and some of my contemporaries — us who fancy ourselves a bit — to admit that we had been worrying ourselves unduly with inessentials, that we had been worrying ourselves to achieve infantile realisms? Well, that day would be a great and disturbing day — for us.

This says everything that Mrs. Woolf said, and a good deal more strongly. We all know the subsequent history; four years after that essay was written, Joyce began the composition of *Ulysses*, and the heyday of the 'infantile realisms' was at an end. But Bennett's anticipatory tribute was generous, and we can be generous to him in return. For now, surely, his period of enforced quarantine is over, his passport is in order, and he should be allowed to land at the harbour of English literature.

(1949–53)

THREE CONTEMPORARY POETS

I. The Reputation of Ezra Pound

FAME, we know, is the last infirmity of noble mind, the illusion we still retain when we have seen through all the others; one rather hopes that Ezra Pound has not discarded all thoughts of fame, and is still capable of being cheered up by them. Because his place in the literary histories, to go no higher, is secure if ever a man's was. Even if posterity takes a low view of his work, he can never be forgotten altogether as long as any records of twentieth-century poetry remain. The worst that can happen to him now is the sort of twilit life we give to a poet like Waller; everyone knows roughly who Waller was and why he was important, and this will continue even though no one reads him.

In his own day, Pound has had two distinct phases of reputation. The first was in his young days, when he was accepted as a mentor (*il miglior fabbro*) by a handful of people — but that handful included the two best poets of the day. We all know the story; Pound induced Mr. Eliot to shorten and concentrate *The Waste Land*; he went over Yeats's poems, rather later, and showed him how to substitute concrete for abstract; Yeats might never have found his mature style if it had not been for Pound's help, or found it much later, having wasted years. Both by the example of his own work, and by his practical advice to others, Pound did more to establish the characteristic English poetry of the twentieth century than anyone else. So much will have to be admitted, in the text-books, for ever; that is what I mean by saying that he can never fall below the Waller bracket of reputation.

And that, at one time, looked like being the whole story; with the 'thirties, a new general style emerged, which had so little in common with the style of the 'twenties that all the observer could say was that it was at any rate not a conservative reaction, not a move back to the pre-war period; one could still, if one didn't like it, say that it was 'modern', just as 'modern' as *The Waste Land*, but that was about all. The new poetry had a common tone and a common aesthetic; where Eliot had tended to make poetry a stern discipline, Auden brought back the tradition of the versifier; ease and fluency were praiseworthy, and a kind of journalistic readiness to write about anything that seemed interesting at the time. Meanwhile Yeats, Eliot, and Pound ('the giant race before the Flood') moved further away from their common centre; Yeats and Eliot ever advancing in greatness, and Pound — one would have said, at the time — sinking into crankiness. He was obviously unfashionable as to subject-matter; his preoccupations seemed to have become a mere network of illusions (such as the idea of getting Mussolini to become a follower of Major Douglas); and as for his literary output, he had got bogged down in the Cantos. This, as I say, was how it evidently looked at the time. Chunks of the Cantos rolled off the assembly-line, which seemed to be stopping and starting a good deal, but nobody could make much of them. Mr. Eliot loyally said that they formed the only long poem by a contemporary which he could read with continuous interest, or words to that effect, but as the others were *The Testament of Beauty* and *The Torchbearers*, this had no very profound effect. With the war, and a third change in the characteristic manner of English poetry, Pound did not move any nearer the centre; his Fascist sympathies, which officially did not affect his poetry one way or the other, did have the effect of making him seem more out of touch than ever; his early poems were still admired, but rather as if they had been the work of a minor genius who had since died or just fizzled out; *Mauberley* was widely taken as an epitaph. 'I was, And I no more exist' — that was about the size of it.

But no one can ever foresee what will happen in literature. After the war, there was a good deal of reconstruction to be done in the arts, and the poet who was just setting out on his life's work had a pretty hard job of selection to do. His first question was the hardest: where was help and technical guidance to come from? I don't mean that people sat about and said in a weak way, 'Who ought we to be influenced by?' — but the fact is that young poets are always influenced by someone; they are lucky if they can create an absolutely individual manner in twenty years of writing, and without the example of someone who has gone over the ground before them, they are usually powerless to start at all. (People who think that poets just *jump* into their art should go back to Chaucer and Shakespeare and examine *their* cases.) It was rather like being confronted with a smashed-up tangle of railway lines and wondering which one to repair first; one had to choose the one that came from somewhere interesting and might be supposed to lead somewhere interesting too. Now, it may be too early, a mere seven or eight years later, to start trying to write the essential literary history of the period; but I think it is pretty clear. The 'thirties were no use, at any rate as far as the main line was concerned, the Auden line; it was worn out even before it got smashed, and what smashed it decisively was not the war but Auden's renunciation of English nationality; after *that* gesture, how could we pretend it was worth going on? His exact contemporaries, those who had stayed here, might have felt committed to pretending it was still open, but that was their problem, not ours. My own answer, which certainly got plenty of support once it was voiced, was that the Empson track was the best one to repair; he had stood rather apart from the others, and had in a way been better placed to inherit the mass of work done by Mr. Eliot, which must always be the true central line of twentieth-century English poetry; Dr. Leavis saw this in *New Bearings*, and if he was rather ungenerous towards the other starters in the field, at least his views had a certain consistency. The Empson boom that followed took me, and I think everyone, by surprise, but at least it showed that there had been some sense in the suggestion that this was the handiest line to repair; certainly the mushy manner of the 'forties, which I thought then and think now was the nadir of English poetry, could not be kept going indefinitely; only Dylan Thomas was big enough to climb out of the morass, and he was an unpredictable genius anyway.

But meanwhile another repair squad, working independently, was busy reconstructing the Pound line. Like the Empson squad, they worked as much from his criticism as from his poetry. They took the whole thing over, lock, stock and barrel; the cosmopolitanism, the multilingual eclecticism, the willingness to pick up the most diverse fragments and bash them together into a 'tradition'. In those days the people concerned were mainly centred on the magazine *Nine* (originally *Seven*), and I still find the files of that paper extraordinarily interesting. What one appreciated was that there wasn't any brawling between the two groups; one's attitude was simply 'Good luck to them if they can make anything of it.' This was the second phase of Pound's reputation, and it is still going on. What comment on it can we fittingly make?

The first, and most, adverse thing to be said is that the revival of interest in him among young men of letters has been accompanied by a too easy acceptance of him by American universities, as a subject for theses. Too easy, because the concrete recommendations that Pound has always made to those engaged in the 'higher' study of literature, are going unregarded as they always did; the man has become a classic — in other words, a nuisance. (It is not so stupid as some of the things we have done over here, of course. One need only remember that the Oxford University Press put Lascelles Abercrombie, a minimal versifier of his day, into the 'Oxford Standard Authors' series *while he was still alive*, and have kept him there ever since! — So much for the literary taste of *our* universities.)

But to come back to Pound: the early phase of his reputation was good because it produced concrete results, and also because it was clear-sighted; it accepted the man at what was, after all, his

own valuation, as an expert verbal mechanic, the literary equi-
valent of the friendly neighbour who straightens up from your
engine with a proud, 'There — I think you'll find she runs better
now.' Eliot and Yeats did find that she ran better, but I have never
heard that they let their gratitude bounce them into making the
same inflated claims for Pound that one hears from his admirers
today. This second generation seem to me to be aware of not
having derived the same practical benefit from their discipleship,
and to be uneasily trying to balance the situation by making more
and larger claims for their hero. They are all quite sure, for instance, that the Cantos are a successful experiment. They believe
in the doctrines put forward in the primers on literature. Some of
them even believe in the social and political theories.

I think we should be nearer the point if we stuck to the view of
Pound as expert verbal mechanic. If there could ever be such a
thing as a stylist pure and simple — a man in whose work style
counted over and above matter — Pound would be that man.
Hence, of course, his fondness for taking some poem in a foreign
language which he doesn't fully understand, brooding over it, and
producing an extraordinarily sensitive reproduction of its tone
and atmosphere. Some queer little streak of obstinacy makes him
refer to these creative broodings as 'translations', and this, of
course, gets him into trouble; but that is beside the point here.
The point is that Pound has emptied himself away to an almost
uncanny degree, leaving the vessel filled with someone else's poem
which he, Pound, has ghost-written for him. Compare these two
snatches:

> Go, Ballatetta, forth and find my Lady,
> Ask if she have it this much of mercy ready,
> This namely, that she turn her eyes toward thee?
> Ask in his name whose whole faith rests in her,
> And if she gracious, this much grace accord thee,
> Offer glad-voiced incense of sweet savour
> Proclaiming of whom thou receiv'st such favour.

That is, of course, the Envoi to one of the Cavalcanti ballades. Now for a bit of 'Chinese'. This one is a complete poem, *Leave-taking Near Shoku*:

> They say the roads of Sanso are steep,
> Sheer as the mountains.
> The walls rise in a man's face,
> Clouds grow out of the hill
>   at his horse's bridle.
> Sweet trees are on the paved way of the Shin,
> Their trunks burst through the paving,
> And freshets are bursting their ice
>   in the midst of Shoku, a proud city.
>
> Men's fates are already set,
> There is no need of asking diviners.

If one didn't know, would one have guessed that these two pieces were by the same writer? I frankly confess, I wouldn't — and for a very obvious reason; that Pound has deliberately cleaned the glass. It is not part of his intention to leave a residue of his own personality in the mixture. But — and this is what I am getting at — it takes a very special kind of poet to be able to do this, and it is here that we approach the possibility of making a fair estimate of Pound's achievement.

Pound is an expert verbal mechanic. I use the expression for the third time. I should like to make it clear just what it means, in terms of art, in terms of helpfulness to others, in terms of permanent value, to be such a thing. Take the two extracts I have quoted. The Cavalcanti one has a restrained sonority, an open and easy strictness, which would be a justification of years of effort if a man did nothing else. (If you think it is easy to write like that, just *try* it.) The Chinese piece, on the other hand, has a seeming casualness into which a tremendous pressure of meaning is packed; dispensing with formal verse, because that tone of deliberate conversation is one of the things that formal verse won't do, it nevertheless goes to work in a very delicate and careful way. The title is an essential part of the poem, since leave-taking is not mentioned explicitly anywhere else; there is also an epigraph, 'Sanso, King of Shoku, built roads'. The friends are taking leave in the pleasant city; one of them (or is it both?) faces the journey to some remote and uncomfortable province, over the mountain roads; it is, if you like, a cliché-situation of Chinese poetry — but how superbly it is caught, with never a drop of its essence spilt! The resignation of the last two lines, emblematic of the kind of thoughts that are running in the heads of the two friends as they turn away from each other, is, I think, perfectly achieved. And it is an achievement absolutely different from that of the Cavalcanti poem.

Any poet who happens to read this article will remember, I am sure, the tremendous catalystic effect that Pound's work had on him when he first met it. That extraordinary blend of the speaking and the singing voice — it was *not* casual, it was *not* just random 'free verse' — even at the age of eighteen one could see that. Wait — I must give myself the pleasure of copying a few lines out.

> Dark eyed,
> O woman of my dreams,
> Ivory sandalled,
> There is none like thee among the dancers,
> None with swift feet.
>
> I have not found thee in the tents,
> In the broken darkness.
> I have not found thee at the well-head
> Among the women with pitchers.
>
> Thine arms are as a young sapling under the bark;
> Thy face as a river with lights.
>
> White as an almond are thy shoulders;
> As new almonds stripped from the husk.
> They guard thee not with eunuchs;
> Not with bars of copper.

And a few pages further on, one would find this:

> Annalists will continue to record Roman reputations,
> Celebrities from the Trans-Caucasus will belaud Roman celebrities
> And expound the distentions of Empire,
> But for something to read in normal circumstances?
> For a few pages brought down from the forked hill unsullied?
> I ask a wreath which will not crush my head,
> And there is no hurry about it;
> I shall have, doubtless, a boom after my funeral,
> Seeing that long standing increases all things regardless of quality.

The one on a Biblical theme has the whole flavour of the Near East about it (I don't mean the Near East as it actually is, but as it exists imaginatively); the language used is a selection from among that of the *Song of Solomon*; while the passage from Propertius is world-weary, metropolitan, ironic. A word like 'distentions', so beautifully used in the second piece, could not imaginably fit into the first. I don't want to labour the point; anyone who considers the two quotations side by side will see what sort of a poet we are dealing with.

Pound has always seen each new poem as a 'job'; something practical to be done, a technical problem to be solved. His criticism is the curt impatience of the man in his shirt-sleeves, waving the theorists to one side. His most withering scorn is reserved for people who are incompetent, who get in the way of those who are trying to do the job. It is significant that Mr. Eliot's remark, 'No *vers* is *libre* for the man who wants to do a good job,' with its oddly uncharacteristic ring, occurs in his preface to Pound's poems; it is a Poundian remark, terse and colloquial. This practical attitude is very catching; Mr. Hugh Kenner, for instance, falls into the same manner in his Introduction to *The Translations of Ezra Pound* (1953). His opening words are as follows:

> Pope translated the *Iliad* into heroic couplets, Chapman into fourteeners. Numerous foreign poems have been shoved into an idiom invented by Milton, which goes flat the moment the atmosphere is cleared of sulphur.

Almost like a parody, isn't it?

'Underlying conspicuous success of the *Seafarer* order is Pound's conception of what the poet's job is,' Mr. Kenner goes on a little later: 'the rendering, without deformation, of something, within him or without, which he has clearly apprehended and seized in his mind. . . . Translating does not, for him, differ in essence from any other poetic job.'

Mr. Kenner has described very accurately, there, Pound's conception of 'the poetic job'. To render, 'without deformation', something which he has firmly grasped in his mind, something 'within him or without'. Notice the almost complete lack of concern with the poetic imagination here; that poetic imagination which makes it hard to say which things are 'within' the poet and which are 'without'. 'Metaphorical language . . . marks the before unapprehended relations of things' — Pound doesn't talk in that strain. To him, and to his disciples, the 'job' is to render something which was already 'apprehended' before the search for expression began.

This leads to a curious lack of interest in what is being *communicated* in a work of literature. For instance, in one of his lists of essential reading, Pound gives 'STENDHAL — at least a book and half'. If, that is, you have got the hang of his method by the time you get half-way through the second book — why then, you're through for the day. Of course this sort of thing is partly a joke, but the insistence on technics is too pervasive to be anything but serious. That is why Pound's lambasting of Milton, for instance, is not seriously damaging; his objection was entirely on stylistic grounds, without any hint that he had even considered the poem's subject-matter, and the complex of ideas and attitudes informing it. If he had, the style might not have seemed such a bad one after all. In Mr. Eliot's case, his early dislike of Milton may have stemmed originally from a Poundian impatience with its manner, but obviously from the start there was an element of Anglo-Catholic reaction against what was *said*.

Is Pound, then, a mere technician? No, because the 'mere' technician cannot exist in art, above the very lowest level of imitativeness. There can be no such thing as a painter who is interested in technique and not in what he is painting; it is a contradiction in terms. Pound comes very close to it, but on due examination he, too, turns out to be interested in something over and above 'style'. And what is it?

Well, what would you expect it to be, in a cosmopolitan American born in the 1880's? Precisely. 'Civilization.' If language is not kept in perfect tune, by a succession of dedicated mechanics, then the thing that will suffer is civilization. Let me quote the eloquent and, I think, moving plea for this case that Pound made in *How To Read* (1931):

> Has literature a function in the state, in the aggregation of humans . . .? It has.
>
> And this function is *not* the coercing or emotionally persuading, or bullying or suppressing people into the acceptance of any one set or any six sets of opinions as opposed to any other one set or half-dozen sets of opinions.
>
> It has to do with the clarity and vigour of 'any and every' thought and opinion. It has to do with maintaining the very cleanliness of the tools, the health of the very matter of thought itself. Save in the rare and limited instances of invention in the plastic arts, or in mathematics, the individual cannot think and communicate his thought, the governor and legislator cannot act effectively or frame his laws, without words, and the solidity and validity of these words is in the care of the damned and despised *literati*. When their work goes rotten — by that I do not mean when they express indecorous thoughts — but when their very medium, the very essence of their work, the application of word to thing goes rotten, *i.e.*, becomes slushy and inexact, or excessive or bloated, the whole machinery of social and of individual thought and order goes to pot. This is a lesson of history, and a lesson not half learned.

One wants to applaud; it is true and needs saying. But is it a lesson half learned? Is it not rather a half-lesson too thoroughly learned? Because, after all, which comes first — the decay of

language as the medium of thought, or the decay in quality of the
living of which that thought is the expression? The whole complex of causes cannot be simplified into a mere piece of immediate give-and-take; 'language is not properly looked after by
the people into whose keeping it is assigned; hence thought goes
rotten; hence judges and legislators lose their grip, and society
collapses'. It is all much too easy, and it is, I am afraid, much too
typical of Pound's thinking on general topics. The Cantos, for
instance, are a collection of magnificent fragments, whose over-
riding object is to recommend certain attitudes. These attitudes
Pound finds in diverse places, in Homer, in Confucius, in Jeffer-
son; and he uses his power as a translator and *pasticheur* — that
power always astonishing, always undiminished — to present us
with a concrete embodiment of them. It is perfectly true that the
Cantos are consistent; but it is not true, I think, that this consistency holds good in an artistic sense. The effect is kaleidoscopic,
and if you are going to be kaleidoscopic in a long poem you cannot, by very definition, be anything else. In fact, I do not think
the Cantos are a single long poem at all; they are merely the
continuation of Pound's fragmentary output, drawing nourishment from any source that seems inviting; if they were given
separate titles and headed, 'The Collected Poems of Ezra Pound',
would it even occur to the critics to find a structure in them?

What helps, of course, to give the Cantos their remarkable
intellectual consistency is that Pound has remained very true to his
own favourite ideas. He has never wavered, for instance, in his
conviction that Confucius is good medicine for the West; in 1931
Confucius was the first name on his list of 'the minimum basis for
a sound and liberal education', with the comment, 'there being no
complete and intelligent English version, one would have either
to learn Chinese or make use of the French version by Pauthier'.
I suppose one might have guessed from that remark that Pound,
if he was spared, would fill this gap himself one day; and sure
enough, twenty-odd years later he gave us a rendering of the 305

M

canonical Odes; a book whose literary merit will not be altered either way by whatever it turns out to be like as a translation, or as a version of Confucianism.

This making a selection from the East is very typical of Pound, and of all his generation of American literary experimenters. They tended to have in common the American refusal to be hampered by mere national frontiers, particularly European ones; to show American impatience at European national differences: much as a lot of American political thinking is dominated by an angry surprise at the fact that, say, Frenchmen think of themselves as different from Spaniards or Italians. Europe is such a small place that it seems odd to find it still further sub-divided into little fragments called 'nations', tenacious of their radically different traditions. Compare, for instance, the imagist manifesto, with its list of the poets who were to be laid under contribution. In *Poetry* for March 1913, when Pound and F. S. Flint enunciated the principles of Imagism, they named Sappho, Catullus, and Villon as principal exemplars; and Pound gave his celebrated recipe:

> Let the candidate fill his mind with the finest cadences he can discover, preferably in a foreign language so that the meaning of the words may be less likely to divert his attention from the movement; *e.g.* Saxon charms, Hebridean Folk Songs, the verse of Dante, and the lyrics of Shakespeare — if he can dissociate the vocabulary from the cadence.

Greek, Latin, Renaissance French, Anglo-Saxon, Elizabethan English — each with its long, dark roots into a complex of thought and lived life — the 'candidate' was expected to pick out a 'cadence' and ignore the rest. The fact that these people belonged to different traditions is something that can easily be got over, in the interests of the poetic 'job'. Louis Macneice tells the story of being in hospital in America at the time of the fall of France, and the nurse saying, 'It's not quite the same for the British — they've got some kind of a gulf over there, haven't they?' 'Some kind of a gulf' was the English Channel; and what she expressed in her naïve way, Pound has expressed, in his life's work, in a more profound and subtle way.

This, together with his preoccupation with the mechanical side of the 'job', has often tended to mislead Pound into producing a bundle of simplifications instead of really thought-out opinions; he has often failed to take account of the actual richness and confusion of human affairs. In the end, however, he has derived part of his impressiveness from this; he has inhabited a cleaner, simpler, and saner world than anything that actually exists, and it is to this world that his poems belong. I do not see how his example can ever cease to be important.

(1955)

II. Ambiguous Gifts: Notes on the Poetry of William Empson

I was sorry to see that the *Sewanee Review*, having occasion in a recent issue to mention William Empson in its 'Notes on Contributors', set him down baldly as 'British critic'. One knew that criticism was a more profitable activity than poetry, but this seems to indicate that it is also more durable. In an age when nine out of ten people who bother about literature do so because they are drawing a salary for it, it may well be that criticism will be read and remembered while poetry is forgotten, for criticism breeds fresh criticism more easily than poetry breeds fresh poetry; but in Empson's case it would be a pity if he were known simply as the 'ambiguity' man, and not as a poet. Of course it is the penalty of silence — he has published nothing in verse since *The Gathering Storm* in 1940 — and in these scribbling days, out of print is out of mind. The position is made all the more difficult by the fact that Empson, as poet no less than as critic, has very firm local associations, and that these associations have themselves ceased to count for much. He was always placed, rightly or wrongly, as a product of the Cambridge English school: certainly the influence of Richards is very evident in *Seven Types*, and the professor repaid his pupil's compliment by quoting his poetry in lectures. What is more, Empson was one of the early contributors to *Scrutiny*, besides being one of the two young poets singled out by Dr. Leavis to be publicly congratulated in *New Bearings* (the other was Ronald Bottrall, who, it seems, has since been sent back to the bottom of the class — see *Scrutiny* for spring 1947). I do not wish to imply that Empson's association with these teacher-critics is any reason why he should be neglected, but when a writer begins his career by closely identifying himself with one particular movement, he is likely to be left high and dry when that movement has spent itself. This is true to some extent of all the poets who were breaking new ground in the 'thirties; the conditions (social, political, and literary) which did so much to form their characteristics, have vanished, leaving them without any source of nourishment, and a little beyond the age at which it is possible to make a major adjustment. It is true that Messrs. Spender, Auden, Day Lewis, and Macneice are still more or less firmly in possession of the public ear, but that is really due to the mediocrity of the younger poetic generation; they are likely to stay in fashion, however little they have to say, simply because their juniors have even less. Still, it is depressing to see poets carrying on from sheer force of habit, and one of the reassuring things about Empson is that, having produced two very remarkable volumes of verse before the rot set in, he has since had the wisdom to hold his peace, even though this means being described in American reviews as 'British critic'.

I shall have some more positive claims to make for Empson's poetry, but first we must see it in its historical setting.

The trouble with the 'thirties, as a literary epoch, is that they happened a long time ago. As I write this I have to keep remembering that Empson is nearly twenty years my senior, and that *Seven Types of Ambiguity* came out when I was just learning to read nursery rhymes. It is thus an act of the historical imagination to discuss such matters as the storm that blew up over the use, in

verse, of the names of machinery and other 'anti-poetic' material
(as if Arthur Hugh Clough, with his fondness for railway imagery,
had not already started it anyway). All one can say at this distance
of time is the obvious thing, that it is useful, like any other
material, when it is properly assimilated, and not lugged along in
the form of compulsory equipment. Many ludicrous failures
could be listed, but they are usually cases where such imagery was
slapped on with a trowel. Take Mr. Day Lewis's lines on the
death of a friend:

> Was so much else we could have better spared —
> Churches, museums, multiple stores: but the bomb
> Fell on the power-house: total that eclipse.
> He was our dynamo, etc. etc.

Here the symbolism is (quite literally) useless; the poet would
have lost nothing by saying simply that the most gay and vital
person of his acquaintance was dead. Empson never jars like this.
He places concrete for abstract in a way that, even in its least
exciting passages, is recognizable as English poetry.

> Law makes long spokes of the short stakes of men.
> Your well fenced out real estate of mind
> No high flat of the nomad citizen
> Looks over, or train leaves behind.

What is more, when he introduces scientific or mechanical
imagery, he does so because it has a genuine function in the poem;
whereas Auden, for instance, is clever at placing such imagery at
the fringe of the poem, where it can do small harm and little good.
When Auden writes

> O all the instruments agree
> The day of his death was a dark, cold day

the *frisson* is really coming from the second line, which might be
as old as *Beowulf*; the bit about the instruments is just there to look
chic and contemporary.

But this question is really part of a bigger one, into which we must go more fully. How far ought scientific ideas to be incorporated into poetry? Poets, from Wordsworth on, have been better at talking about the relevance of science than actually doing anything about it, and this seems to be one of the ways in which Empson has made a real advance. It is worth noticing that in both prose and verse his mind flies to the scientific for analogy and metaphor. In his prose it is merely irritating. *Seven Types* is not really impregnated with the scientific spirit, despite its title; it is a collection of *aperçus* based on a method of analysis inaugurated by Riding and Graves in *Survey of Modernist Poetry*. But the reek of the laboratory was so strong in the author's nostrils as he wrote that we have to endure a barrage of not very illuminating asides like 'Here as in recent atomic physics there is a shift in progress' or 'having fixed the reaction, properly stained, on a slide, they must be able to turn the microscope on it with a certain indifference and without smudging it with their fingers'. In *Some Versions of Pastoral* we are even told that 'Milton's evasive use of language ... has the squalid gelatinous effect of ectoplasm in a flashlight photograph'. At all events this is probably not a mere affectation, since Empson started as a mathematician and probably knows a certain amount of science as well; but in the attempt to bring scientific ideas into poetry, it is not enough to know what you are talking about. James Thomson had read up quite a lot of eighteenth-century physics, but when he came to introduce it into *The Seasons* the result is rather forced.

> What art thou, frost? — and whence are thy keen stores
> Derived, thou secret all-invading power,
> Whom even the illusive fluid cannot fly?
> Is not thy potent energy, unseen,
> Myriads of little salts, or hooked, or shaped
> Like double wedges, and diffused immense
> Through water, earth, and ether?

Who cares? The fact is that it is useless merely to *describe* in verse the things of which science tells us, while to introduce them in the form of simile and metaphor when the poem is really about something quite non-scientific is not much better. The only way to treat such material is to form it into a series of conceits on which the general meaning of the poem can be made to turn. This was Donne's way, and it is Empson's. In *The World's End* he uses the perfectly straightforward idea that, since space is 'curved', there is no such thing as the end of the world; you are always beginning your journey afresh, and so the world is a more oppressive prison than you ever suspected.

> Apples of knowledge and forgetful mere
> From Tantalus too differential bend.
> The shadow clings. The world's end is here.

In the same way *Arachne* is not really about either soap-tension, or molecular structure, or the habits of water-spiders. These things are pivots on which a tragically sardonic love-poem is made to turn; the whole thing is a triumphant *tour de force* which culminates with a simultaneous application of all the available symbols to a pair of human lovers:

> We two suffice. But oh beware, whose vain
> Hydroptic soap my meagre water saves.
> Male spiders must not be too early slain.

Empson wrote this poem at, or before, the age of twenty-three (he was born in 1906 and this appeared in *Cambridge Poetry* 1929); and even those who are not attracted to the poem — it can be found in *The Oxford Book of Modern Verse* — will agree that to express such a complexity of ideas in a metre as tight as *terza rima*, and in language entirely suited to its purpose, is a good enough start for a poetic career.

Another distant echo from the past is the question of 'obscurity'. Nowadays one of two things will generally happen; either a poem will offer little or no difficulty, because its readers have grown up reading that kind of poetry and do not have to make the awkward crossing from one kind of reading to another; or it may be really obscure, in the bad sense, because the poet does not want to be understood, in which case no one will find it worth the effort to protest. As regards prose, where obscurity really is intolerable, Cyril Connolly's remark seems all that is required: 'A writer who thinks himself cleverer than his readers will write simply, one who is afraid they are cleverer than he, will make use of mystification; good style is arrived at when the language chosen represents what the author requires of it without shyness.' As regards verse, the issue is not so simple. For one thing, the author is not always so certain what it is that he is requiring of his language: he is giving the wagon a push to see how far it will roll by itself. This sounds dangerously close to a defence of 'romanticism' in the bad sense, or even a rationalization of automatic writing, but in reality it is true even of the poet with a firm intellectual grasp — indeed it is precisely this that makes such a grasp necessary. It is harder to produce an accurate statement than a careless rapture, harder still to combine the two, yet poetry *is* this combination. Tired of it though we all are, the question of 'obscurity' forces itself on our attention in discussing a poet whose blurb describes him as 'the most brilliantly obscure of modern poets': unfortunately Empson's own statement on the subject is itself of uncertain significance. In his Note on the Notes to *The Gathering Storm* he says, 'partly they are meant to be like answers to a crossword puzzle; a sort of puzzle interest is part of the pleasure you are meant to get from the verse, and that I get myself when I go back to it.' Obviously this is not wholly serious, any more than the Preface to Graves's *Poems 1938–45*, about the islanders who took in each other's washing, is wholly serious; but neither is a good enough joke to be that and nothing more. One has to take Empson's remark about puzzles at least partly in good faith, because it really represents a feature of his mind; a 'puzzle interest' is evidently part of the pleasure he gets from all poetry.

Some Versions is constantly saying this; 'Milton's language about stars contains two puzzles about them', the Darwinian passages in *Alice in Wonderland* are 'tantalizing', and so forth. Indeed, his two books of criticism are valuable chiefly as a very telling attack on the idea that we understand what we read.

In any case, it is usually best to obey any instructions from a poet as to how his work should be approached. If Empson's work is advertised as 'obscure', and he himself speaks of 'puzzle-interest', it would obviously be dishonest in a critic not to make some attempt to see what this means in practice. As a specimen of his more cryptic vein, I here quote in full *The Teasers* (*Gathering Storm*, p. 38).

> Not but they die, the teasers and the dreams,
> Not but they die,
> > and tell the careful flood
> To give them what they clamour for and why.
>
> You could not fancy where they rip to blood,
> You could not fancy
> > nor that mud
> I have heard speak that will not cake or dry.
>
> Our claims to act appear so small to these,
> Our claims to act
> > colder lunacies
> That cheat the love, the moment, the small fact.
>
> Make no escape because they flash and die,
> Make no escape
> > build up your love,
> Leave what you die for and be safe to die.

To begin with the form: it is a blend of originality and imperfection. The first stanza suggests a real lyrical discovery — a metre one does not remember to have seen elsewhere, and a beautiful one. The rhyme scheme, *dreams — die — flood — why*, is a normal quatrain which justifies the broken second line. The second stanza goes one better with *blood — fancy — mud — dry*, which is stricter, and moreover carries on the rhyme from *flood* in a way that suggests *terza rima*. Stanza 3 carries on the improved form well, though no further effort is made to carry on a rhyme from the preceding stanza; but the whole thing crumbles in the fourth with a lame *die — escape — love — die*. The form, in fact, is typically Empsonian: the brilliant discovery of a minor verse-form which exactly suits its content, and then the uncertainty which keeps him swinging between unresolved possibilities, and finally the collapse into random shapelessness. As with rhyme, so with metre. The second line, a decasyllabic in stanza 1, octosyllabic in stanza 2, shapeless nothing in stanza 3, and octosyllabic again in stanza 4. Does this matter? Emphatically yes, in a lyric poem twelve lines long. For one thing, it renders the whole poem suspect. Is it worth trying to decipher the meaning of a poet who is so little interested in the problem of expressing himself that he cannot be bothered to sustain a simple metrical form for four stanzas together?

Now for this 'meaning'. When people refuse to talk about the 'meaning' of a poem, in the sense of its paraphrasable content, I take it that what they are objecting to is the idea that a poem has one meaning (the 'right' one) and no other. Nowadays we have reached such a pitch of sophistication that no one would confess to so naïve a view: each reader makes his own poem, we assure each other, on the basis of the words provided for him by the poet. This would be all very well if it did not lead to so widespread a neglect of a poem's paraphrasable content; the feeling seems to be that if this content is different to each reader, there is no point in bothering about it: whereas of course the mere fact that a poem varies from reader to reader makes it all the more imperative for each reader to work out for himself the exact 'meaning' of every poem he comes across. One risks a lot by coming into the open on matters like these, but here is my paraphrase of the poem in question.

The teasers and dreams are our inward afflictions and aspirations — in Bacon's noble phrase, the 'desires of the mind'. These desires, though they die and are merged with the undiscriminating stream of existence ('the careful flood' — possibly with an underlying reference to Styx) are still so much more important than the 'colder lunacies' — the disciplined and regulated actions — that it is useless to try to evade them (rendering l. 13 as 'do not, merely because they flash and die, seek to escape them'). Grouped about this hub of meanings is a riot of subsidiary meanings; to enumerate them would be a lengthy business and best done afresh by each reader. The second stanza, for example, seems to rely wholly on suggestion, and it is possible to deduce (or devise) at least a dozen 'logical' meanings for it, but its function seems to be more like that of a simile or metaphor: intensification and, in a roundabout way, illustration. The poem appears to collapse into negation in the last stanza; if you abandon what you would normally be defending, you will be safe — to die, i.e. you will gain nothing. I shall be told, of course, that I have entirely missed the point, but it were better to be wrong than to follow the common critical practice of refusing to make the attempt. Besides which, the poem is not mentioned in the Notes which occupy sixteen pages of the volume, and must therefore be assumed to lie at the mercy of the reader.

Partly for the reasons I have given, Empson has often been called 'metaphysical'; and on this side, too, his work needs some historical comment.

During the last twenty-five years the seventeenth century has been much in the air, and apologists for 'modern' poetry have found the appeal to Donne and the late Shakespeare a very useful weapon (we are not forced, like the French, to choose finally between the present and the past in our poetic theory). Yet, while it is legitimate to defend intellectualized and elliptical poetry by calling on the 'metaphysicals', the theory is, after all, propaganda, and must be modified when the shouting has died down. This, evidently, is not yet: in 1948 English reviewers could still hail Cleanth Brooks's ten-year-old *Modern Poetry and the Tradition*, which argues along these lines, as if it were the last word on its subject. How much twentieth-century poetry, examined in cold blood, really resembles Donne or Marvell? I should say that only John Crowe Ransom, Robert Graves since 1926, and possibly the early dandified Eliot, ever consistently recalled the metaphysical way of setting about poetry. Whether the theory about 'dissociation of sensibility' is true or not, that particular blend of thinking and feeling has been very rare since 1700, and the claim that it has been revived in our own time does not bear much examination: Auden, for instance, has not been blending them at all, but slipping from one to the other — hence the utter lack of repose and certainty even in his best work. For the rest, there are a few traces of Donne, but generally through one of the conventional intermediaries — Hopkins, Browning, Eliot himself — and there the matter rests. So that, historically speaking, the renascence of (in any precise sense of the word) 'metaphysical' poetry boils down to a few poems by a few poets.

Empson, however, is one of these poets. It is not easy to define metaphysical poetry, but obviously there are two features which distinguish it at once — a kind of general modernity which leads poets to bring in current ideas and current language, and a strong, at times almost perverse, desire to follow the argument wherever it leads the poem. Donne's poetry has no more 'conceits' in it than anyone else's, but the conceits are taken seriously and allowed to lead the poem from one point to another. It is this trait which links Empson most firmly to the seventeenth century. Witness the pursuit of the idea in these lines:

> All those large dreams by which men long live well
> Are magic-lanterned on the smoke of hell;
>   This then is real, I have implied,
>   A painted, small, transparent slide.

These the inventive can hand-paint at leisure,
Or most emporia would stock our measure;
    And feasting in their dappled shade
    We should forget how they were made.

And so the argument goes on developing until, like some great glittering, tortured poem of Donne or Crashaw, it seals our assent with the measured rhetoric of the last stanza.

Imagine, then, by miracle, with me
(Ambiguous gifts, as what gods give must be),
    What could not possibly be there,
    And learn a style from a despair.

I speak of 'measured rhetoric'; and indeed it would be impossible to assess Empson's achievement without some reference to the slow, heavy fulness of his lines; they seem to me a miraculous blend of the colloquial immediacy of Donne and the immense weight of Hopkins; and in the middle of a quiet, meditative poem he will suddenly introduce lines of an enormous Marlovian grandeur —

Wait, to be fathered as was Bacchus once,
Through men's long lives, that image of time's end.

Of course no landscape is made up entirely of peaks; Empson has published, even in his small output, a number of pieces that are too slight to be worth sustained attention — *Just a Smack at Auden* and *Your Teeth are Ivory Towers* would be good if made up extempore at a party — while

This passive style might pass perhaps
Squatting in England with the beer,
But if that's all you think of, what
In God's name are you doing here?

is a little too prattling. At the other end of the scale is the over-elaboration of a poem like *Bacchus*, which requires six pages of notes ('A mythological chemical operation to distil drink is going on in the first four verses') and seems hardly worth the fuss. But he has, after all, written at least a dozen poems which pass every known test of greatness: and who has done more?

Whether Empson will ever write any more poetry is not my business. If he does, it will be interesting to see whether the land-slide in English literary taste has left us with a public capable of appreciating him. For the plain fact is that many of the reputations which today occupy the poetic limelight are such as would crumble immediately if poetry such as Empson's, with its passion, logic, and formal beauty, were to become widely known. If the day ever comes when poems like *This Last Pain*, *To an Old Lady*, *Manchouli*, *Note on Local Flora*, are read and pondered, and their lessons heeded, it will be a sad day for many of our punch-drunk random 'romantic' scribblers. But I suppose it never will.

(1949)

III. DYLAN THOMAS: A REVIEW OF HIS COLLECTED POEMS[1]

Reviewing this volume is not, in the ordinary sense, reviewing at all. Here are the poems we have all been familiar with for years, which have been explored, acclaimed, damned, rejected and worshipped throughout the entire adult life of anyone aged less than thirty-five; and 'reviewing' them is merely a matter of passing them round and giving each critic an opportunity to say where he, personally, stands with regard to Mr. Thomas's work.

Most people have said their say by now; this would be, if one could be bothered, a good opportunity to survey the kind of thing that has been said. But I doubt if any such summary could, at this stage, be useful or entertaining: most kinds of critical mistakes have been made in dealing with these poems, and will no doubt go on being made, and that is about all there is to it. The

[1] Dylan Thomas, *Collected Poems*, 1934–52.

wild overpraise of Thomas's original backers was answered by the savage onslaught of those who felt that the whole thing had gone too far, and by about 1946 one felt that the critics were quite simply talking to each other rather than the public, and certainly not bothering overmuch about the poems. The small-arms fire has now grown so hot that anyone who shows his head is sure to be riddled from some quarter: for instance, Mr. Read's famous 'these poems cannot be reviewed: they can only be acclaimed' (of *Twenty-Five Poems*) drew such furious abuse and raillery that nowadays no one dare be so outspoken, even if they feel really strongly impelled to praise Thomas; and so one finds, for instance, a Sunday reviewer saying that 'it need no longer be eccentric' to say that Thomas is the greatest living writer of English poetry. What he meant was that he thought so himself, but did not dare say so outright in case some anti-Thomas bully came round to thrash him, so had to dress it up with a meaningless qualification. In that particular case, of course, it is unnecessary to do more than say No; it is, clearly, eccentric, not to say imperceptive, to call Thomas the greatest living writer of English verse as long as Eliot is still writing, to say nothing of Auden, Graves and several others. At the other extreme we have the disgraceful treatment of Thomas in *Scrutiny*, which is, I am afraid, only typical of that magazine's bad record over contemporary poetry in general. It is rather significant that the best review of this collection should have appeared in the *New Statesman* — a paper for whose criticism *Scrutiny* can never say a good word.

But I must get on with the job, which is to say briefly (for what it is worth) where I stand on the Thomas question. I think, then, that he is a fine, bold, original and strong poet whose work is marred by two great drawbacks. First, a disastrously limited subject-matter. There are really only three subjects treated: (i) childhood, and the associated topic of what it is like to remember one's childhood; (ii) the viscera; (iii) religion. The first is very well handled, but really nobody could improve on the *Portrait of*

the Artist as a Young Dog as saying all that can be said about growing up, and if you add the related group of verse pieces, chiefly the
quasi-Wordsworthian *Poem in October*, you really find that there
is nothing left to do. The second, the viscera, is of course an
important subject, and the early poems with their obsessive concern with anatomy and crude physical sensation are fine and
valuable poems, but here again you can say the last word, and say
it pretty quickly. Thomas has added almost no good love poetry
to the language, because he always seems to treat sexual love as an
affair of glandular secretions and the mingling of fluids, which is
only true as far as it goes. The third subject, religion, seems to me
Thomas's worst pitch; he never succeeds in making me feel that
he is doing more than thumbing a lift from it. Indeed it is only a
helpful subject to him in those poems which are content to leave
every important matter to be settled by the reader: the line 'After
the first death, there is no other', has been praised as an example of
significant ambiguity (either 'when you are dead there's an end of
it' or 'after this mortal life comes the eternal one'), and no doubt
that is very valuable, but if a poet is going to be a religious
poet there has (one would think) to be a little more definition
about it.

   This leads on to the second great flaw which keeps Thomas's
poetry at a remove from greatness: the suspicion (which has,
goodness knows, been voiced often enough) that his writing, in
the more 'difficult' poems, is quasi-automatic. It is perfectly
possible to furnish even his wildest pieces with a 'meaning' (*i.e.* a
paraphrasable content or set of alternative paraphrasable contents), but the gnawing doubt remains as to whether the writer
really *cared* whether it meant anything precise or not. This, of
course, is the great point that has to be settled; not until every
one of the more obscure poems has been thoroughly thrashed out
(as, in time, they will be) can we feel confident of reaching an
answer. Meanwhile we want a little less gas about Thomas, and
some criticism that really talks turkey and gets down to particular

instances. The thing is, meanwhile, very worrying to the honest reader. Take, for instance, the line

And I am struck as lonely as a holy maker by the sun.

Why does the sun strike a holy maker lonely? Or rather, to put first things first, does it just strike the poet lonely, as lonely as a holy maker? Of course a holy maker is lonely, whether the expression means (i) a specifically religious poet, (ii) just any poet ('all makers are holy'), (iii) God. This third suggestion comes from a friend who said it was 'obvious' that the line referred to God creating the sun, and feeling lonely because for the first time there existed in the universe something with which it was possible to have a relationship, and therefore the concept of loneliness appeared. But if so, why 'a' holy maker and not 'the'? At this point, does one plunge ahead, hoping to reach the further shore, or does one simply go back in despair and say that the effect is of a latter-day Swinburne who just wants to make a nice noise? Answers to these and all the other questions of interpretation are easy to supply; but (and this is the point) they are not easy to cleanse, when supplied, of a certain *voulu* or factitious quality.

This, by the way, would be the place for a few remarks in contradiction of one of the most obstinate absurdities that bedevil discussion of this poet: the idea, brought up on occasion by his supporters and opponents alike, that he is a divinely inspired simpleton; what Mr. Eliot, speaking of Blake, called 'a wild pet for the super-cultivated'. His association in the public mind with Miss Sitwell, who is simply not interested in the ordinary processes of being intelligent, has helped to put this nonsense about, but it is obvious to anyone who reads the poems carefully that Thomas puts into them a good deal of ordinary common-or-garden cleverness and capability of the breadwinning, examination-passing type, not a fanciful fourth-dimensional 'poetic' afflatus. This is clear from the very great skill with which he has assimilated his literary influences, the chief of which are, of

N

course, Hopkins and Yeats, though there is a noticeable streak of William Empson (cleverly combined with the Yeats influence in one of the new poems here, the villanelle). Thomas is also a brilliant parodist, another sure test of acuteness of the ordinary day-to-day type (no fool ever wrote a successful parody even if, which I doubt, a fool ever wrote a successful poem).

To turn definitely to the credit side, there is, of course, all the obvious — magnificently and overwhelmingly obvious — grandeur, generosity and harmony of these poems. The superb balance of rhymes in *The Conversation of Prayer*, for instance, is something to be grateful for; doubly so when one thinks that Thomas came of literary age at a time when the typical successful poet was getting away with lines like these:

> You who go out alone, on tandem or on pillion,
> Down arterial roads riding in April,
> Or sad beside lakes where hill-slopes are reflected
> Making fires of leaves, your high hopes fallen:
> Cyclists and hikers in company, day excursionists,
> Refugees from cursed towns and devastated areas;
> Know you seek a new world, a saviour to establish
> Long-lost kinship and restore the blood's fulfilment.

Compare:

> Once it was the colour of saying
> Soaked my table the uglier side of a hill
> With a capsized field where a school sat still
> And a black and white patch of girls grew playing;
> The gentle seaslides of saying I must undo
> That all the charmingly drowned arise to cockcrow and kill.

If the Thomas passage shows the tendency towards over-richness and artfulness (the field is 'capsized' because there is a school sitting still in it, and schoolboys wear caps, as well as because it is tilted on the side of a hill), one forgives it at once by comparison with the utter nullity of the other extract, which incidentally I chose from an anthology and did not ferret out from among the author's early and buried work. In the criticism of contemporary literature, one's standards are bound to be, essentially, comparative; we cannot know what will interest posterity, but that Thomas's poems will continue to interest the men of his own time cannot be questioned and need not, certainly, be grudged.

(1953)

THE LITERARY CRITIC IN THE
UNIVERSITY

The tutor of a young Roman of good family was usually a slave. A rich man would have a Greek slave as librarian, and slave secretaries and learned men. He would keep his poet as he would keep a performing dog. In this atmosphere of slavery the traditions of modern literary scholarship and criticism, meticulous, timid and quarrelsome, were evolved. — H. G. Wells, *A Short History of the World*, cap. xxxv.

We have the liberal arts and we have the useful arts. This is one of the useful arts. — I will try to learn it, said Stephen. — *A Portrait of the Artist as a Young Man.*

IN a way I suppose I am a parasite on this number of the magazine, as I have just resigned from the post I have held, for eight years, at a university of the kind that is being discussed.[1] Still, as I write, it is not yet quarter day, so that I am still legally on the strength, and in any case I feel it gives my remarks a kind of documentary value, even a certain impressiveness like the words of a dying man. It was my job to teach English literature, and I thought of myself, on the whole, as a kind of resident literary critic; I wasn't interested in 'research', and did not imagine that I was there to train the next generation of professional scholars; neither, on the other hand, did I try to work the stunt about having a special line because I was a 'creative writer'. I thought that having published poems and novels had nothing to do, one way or the other, with my effectiveness as a teacher of English literature. I thought I was there as a critic, to teach people how to be critics. Towards the end, however, I began to see that I was mistaken, and that there is in fact no place for the literary critic in the university.

Let me warn the reader that I am writing in no spirit of flippant paradox. Mr. A. Alvarez wrote an article in these pages, not long ago, about 'The Poet in the University', in which he treated the subject rather like the snakes in Ireland; he said there were no poets in universities, and couldn't be, and that if any poets went to

[1] Written for the 'Redbrick number' of *The Twentieth Century*.

work in universities they ceased to be poets before long. This must have been comforting to all those poets (and there are quite a lot of them) who take up university teaching posts, and find after a few years that their imaginative lava ceases to flow; with Mr. Alvarez to back them, they can blame it on the job; they are relieved of the responsibility. Their talent has died, but at least they did not murder it themselves; if it had not been for having to earn a living (they can now boast) they would have been poets too, and very fine ones. Whether he teaches 'creative writing' (in America), or formal literary history (in England), such a person, we learn, will never write poetry again: 'Either way,' writes Mr. Alvarez, 'he is a middle-man to art, which a really creative artist can never be.' I shall not take this line about critics; criticism is not an art — or rather, it is, but it is one of the useful arts, not one of the fine arts, and it can be carried on by anyone with a certain amount of common sense who is prepared to put himself through a rather long training. My point is that the university cannot *teach* criticism, and that a man employed to talk about literature in such an institution is employed as a teacher, not as a critic.

Literary criticism is the discussion, between equals, of works of literature, with a view to establishing common ground on which judgements of value can be based. As a definition, that is not particularly elegant; it can be rephrased, altered here and there, stood on its head, but it cannot be thrown away altogether. Literary criticism is that, or it is nothing. It is between 'equals' because the essence of all critical discussion is that the participants start fair; if I am describing to you the contents of a book which I have read but you have not, I might talk very interestingly, but I could not even touch the skirts of criticism — or, if I did, that part of my discourse would be solipsism. And the object, in the end, is the judgement of value, and the establishment of a hierarchy of quality; this book *is* better than that one, on grounds that we can, more or less, state; everything is *not* just a matter of individual 'taste'; if we agree that I like *Hamlet* and you like Agatha Christie, we have *not* said the last significant word on the subject. Literary judgements cannot be proved, but they can be debated, and a certain amount of evidence can be called in; discrimination need not be a mere matter of random impulse. George Orwell remarked, 'As a rule, an aesthetic preference is either something inexplicable or it is so corrupted by non-aesthetic motives as to make one wonder whether the whole of literary criticism is not a huge network of humbug.' This is one of the very few silly things that Orwell said, and it is to his credit that his silliness stands out very obviously because it is stated openly and frankly, in plain language, and not wrapped up in evasions. Notice that he thinks literary criticism entirely a matter of stating and defending one's 'aesthetic preferences', whereas of course the reaction to a work of literature is something involving the whole man, of whom the aesthetic is only one part; also, 'aesthetic preferences' are interestingly involved in other parts of the whole person, but this is not the same as saying that they are 'corrupted' by this involvement. Yes, it is easy to make hay of Orwell's statement, but my point is that much of the most fashionable and influential writing about literature, done by academics, is based on exactly the same set of muddles. If you try to find out which academic critics have been heard of by the outside world, and then go and look up their works, you will find them nearly all belonging to the anti-critical, 'fine writing' tradition. Their colleagues, who have not been heard of outside the university, but are still very influential, are generally engaged (if they are engaged in anything) in heaping up facts *about* literature; this is very proper, but again it has nothing, or nothing much, to do with criticism. In fact, it is rather chastening to pause and reflect how many people who write about literature, and are frequently or usually described as 'critics', have never in their lives written a line of criticism as I have described it above. They have imparted information; they have recommended this or that book to their readers or hearers; they have described the contents of books which they are alone in having read; but for the disinterested egalitarian discussion which alone can be called 'criticism', they have no stomach.

We should not, in any case, expect too much. Universities are institutions of learning, and learned men are quite often shockingly indifferent to matters of discrimination. They have other qualities — enthusiasm for their subject, physical stamina which enables them to spend long years in study, an appetite for detail and an admirable gift for undertaking boring work without being bored. But these are not necessarily the qualities of a literary critic, and the record of dons as critics, from Bentley to the present day, is not a good one. We need not flog this dead horse, but I believe that when someone writes a thesis (as someone assuredly will) on 'The Academic Reaction Against Contemporary Poetry in the Twentieth Century', some pretty shocking things will be quoted. It is perhaps right for academic people to be conservative in their tastes; society gives them the rôle of guardians of tradition, and it is natural that they should, if anything, over-stress the virtue of 'a continuous literary decorum'; but there can be no excuse for their habit of spitting at almost every major contemporary poet. This is particularly so as the sniping was nearly always done from hiding-places; most of the attacks on 'modern poetry' were launched in sneering footnotes. A sad example (sad because it is distasteful to have to remember anything to the discredit of a good and learned man) is to be found on p. 73 of Gavin Bone's *Anglo-Saxon Poetry* (Oxford, 1943), an excellent book of translations, very sensitively done. Bone is dealing with rival theories of translation, and he mentions the anti-Gilbert Murray views expressed by 'an American critic, Mr. T. S. Eliot.' Now this sort of thing is just silly impertinence; the insult lies in (i) assuming that Eliot needs identifying at all; (ii) calling him a critic, as if he were the author of some half-forgotten essay and nothing else; (iii) calling him an American, which in the context is a gibe — it means 'an outsider from a commercial civilization who doesn't understand people like Gilbert Murray and myself.' Bone knew perfectly well that by this time Mr. Eliot had been acknowledged for twenty years as a major poet, and knew, for that matter, that he had become a British subject years previously. But the candidate for High-Tableship, bent on picking up the right attitudes along with the right mannerisms, learnt to echo this kind of thing. Finally, of course, uncritical condemnation ended in uncritical acceptance; the average don, feeling that all 'modern' poetry was the same anyway, passed quite naturally from scoffing at Mr. Eliot to accepting utterly invalid reputations and welcoming their bearers into positions of influence. It pains me to put all this down; I rather like dons and some of them are among my best friends, like Jews, but I have to admit that they have not been, in my time, the guardians of a 'continuous literary decorum' in any sense in which I understand the term.

It will be said that literary matters are not one of the University's vital concerns, that literary criticism could be altogether absent from the academic climate and yet it might still be healthy. I cannot feel this; a large proportion of the undergraduates, at any given moment, are studying literature, and it is these people, after they go down, who will become the 'reading public' at its higher level, and who will get the literature they deserve. From this point of view it is nothing short of frightening that so many of the teachers concerned with literature, in the last thirty years, have failed to make any kind of adjustment to the best work that was being produced in the world they and their pupils were actually living in. I remember a very famous old professor, who had been influential in 'Inglit' circles for about forty years, saying that he had been to America, and the students there had asked him what he thought of the poetry of T. S. Eliot, and he had replied (no doubt looking at them roguishly), 'I don't think about it at all.' This was told as a conventionally 'shocking' story; what a wonderfully independent-minded old man, you were meant to think, not to be swept away by the latest craze. Unfortunately, it may be that those American students were familiar with Allen Tate's remark, 'The scholar who tells us that he understands Dryden but makes nothing of Yeats or Hopkins is telling us that he does not understand Dryden.' If a man sets out to interpret the taste of 1660 through the medium of the taste of 1860, he will talk very interestingly, but the result will be something that can only be 'caviary to the general'; young students, reading the literature of the past for the first time, need someone who will interpret its significances in terms of the world *they* are living in, not the world their grandparents lived in. Nor is it a question of age; the problem is not solved by turning away all the old men and giving all the teaching to people under forty; everyone who has moved in university circles knows that your don is very often *born* with this conviction that (as someone put it) Art ceased about the time his mother got married.

It is no use grumbling too much; this is the material we have to work with; and since dons elect one another, they will naturally take care not to alter it. (To ask the opinion of professors on university reforms is like asking the opinion of generals about conscription; we cannot expect anyone to be so candid as to talk himself out of a job.) The only conclusion, I think, is not to expect too much of our literary schools; we must not expect, for instance, English faculties to produce critics of English literature; at best they can only produce people who might, in time, become capable of criticism. It is better to aim at something you can achieve; to teach English literature as a source of essential social history (what it was *like* to live at such-and-such a time), and to give people a grounding in elementary linguistic history, so that they can at any rate *construe* the texts they are reading. I simply do not think that criticism can be taught at this level; it depends on the pupil's having an equal familiarity with the books discussed, and also with the nature of life itself; and of course if they had this familiarity they would not be there. You don't go to lectures given by someone who knows no more than yourself. The university teacher is there because he *knows* more than his students;

only secondarily because he is a critic, because he can discriminate better than they can — for this discrimination is something that he cannot, in any case, teach them.

The difference between Oxford and Cambridge comes in here. When I was an Oxford undergraduate I was taught simple appreciation; I read an enormous number of authors, in rapid succession, and in each case I learnt to pick out what could be 'said for' the man. Nobody taught me, as Cambridge undergraduates seem to be taught, that every author has to get through a kind of sieve, called Criticism, before he is considered worth reading. All the time that Oxford spends in learning the difference between one Middle English dialect and another, Cambridge spends in constructing this sieve, which — at that age, and with that equipment — can only mean learning a special patter. I doubt the usefulness of this. I have often heard it said, though more often at Cambridge than at Oxford, that the business of an English School is not to produce writers, but to produce critics; but I think we are lucky if, by the time they are twenty-two, we have got them to the stage where they can begin, painfully, to turn themselves into either. At all events, my experience has been that a literary critic who works at a university, and spends himself in the effort to teach *criticism*, sets himself a cripplingly hard task and has, after all, disappointingly little more to show for it than his colleagues who have taken life easily. His pupils will have a good line in patter, because — and this is the unfortunate thing — the methods and attitudes of a critic, like those of an artist, are susceptible of imitation; great fleas have little fleas upon their backs to bite 'em, no less in criticism than in art, and a young man of genuine ability, who was schooled by a critic of definite opinions and formed attitudes, might find himself faced with an 'agonizing reappraisal' indeed; he would have to hack his way back to a point from which he could begin again, and in the end it would have been kinder to teach him a few simple facts than to try to turn him into a critic. That phrase 'a few simple facts' will no doubt be scoffed at a good deal, so I ought to repeat that I mean just that; I mean a few, I mean simple and I mean facts. I would rather have a youth of twenty-two able to construe a few pages of Chaucer, or explain the references in fifty lines of *Paradise Lost*, than turn out any amount of 'discrimination' which he had picked up from someone else. The job of a university teacher, in English literature, is — as I see it — to take people at a walking pace through the major works of the English tradition and see that they have some inkling of what the authors thought they were saying. Clever stuff about what they were *really* saying, and exactly why one is preferable to another, can come later.

I now want to say a word about this 'later'. It is nowadays increasingly the fashion for young men to stay at the university after they have finished their first degree; the university teacher without a doctorate, or at any rate a second degree of some kind, is becoming rare. It is, I suppose, all part of our increasing Americanization. Nevertheless, it cannot just be shrugged off as a fad. If — to take one representative figure — there are a hundred people doing 'research' into English literature at Oxford, it is a matter of some general concern to find out exactly what they are doing and whether that amount of energy could be used more profitably. I do not propose to tackle this subject myself, because anything I said would simply be brushed aside as lacking sufficient weight, but from the point of view of my chosen subject here — the literary critic in the university — there is one word I ought to say. Would it not be possible (I ask very humbly, ready to be ignored) for the practice of literary criticism to be encouraged among this army of fresh, energetic young men, not yet staled and blunted by years of donkey-work? Is it an immutable law of nature that they *must* give up this fruitful and formative period of their lives to the study of the minutiæ of literary history?

I am only asking. I know research is important, and I should be the last to hinder any young man, or any old man for that matter, who had said to himself, 'This problem seems to me very important. The progress of my thinking in this matter depends on my getting it settled; I am interested in nothing else until I have dug deep enough to solve the problem and any others that turn out to be related.' This I respect. But the endless whine of, 'Suggest something for me to research on', which one hears all day long at all our universities, strikes me as very little short of contemptible. Unless and until there is a problem really on your mind, you have no business to undertake research, unless of course you have the money to be able to please yourself, which nobody nowadays has. 'Ah, but it is done to teach *method*.' At this sacred word, I suppose, we are all to prostrate ourselves. 'Dull men taught craft are merely dull with aplomb,' Mr. Alvarez tersely remarked in his article; and, if I may paraphrase, nitwits who are taught method are merely nitwits with more power to their elbows; they will insinuate themselves into responsible positions and spread the blight of their own incomprehension for forty years among the young. Jack Smith, who scrapes a second in the Schools and is known as an amiable bore, is under control; but teach him enough 'method' and he will be Doctor J. Smith, famed for his researches.[1] English literature is already bespattered with footnotes about 'Professor So-and-so, to whom we owe our knowledge of Akenside's birthplace.' (We all thought he had been born at Number 12, Market Place, but now it turns out to have been Number 13.) Much of the criticism levelled at learned 'research' is based on an ignorance of what is really needed; a thesis that strikes the layman as foolishly *recherché* might well provide the vital link in some important chain; but for the love of Mike let us scrap this argument about 'method'. If a man wants to find something out, he will find it out. Who taught Thomas Warton method? Or Warburton, or Johnson, or Theobald? When Bertram Dobell discovered and identified those manuscripts of Traherne, which I take to be the greatest literary dis-

---

[1] If there really is someone called Jack Smith, I assure him I don't mean *him*.

covery of this century, did he owe his ability to having been taught method?

Humbly, therefore, I return again to the central issue. Bowing from the waist, I ask a question. Would it not be possible for some of the young men who take further degrees to write *a critical essay* on the author or subject of their choice? An essay that had no necessary connection with 'research', save perhaps in the sense intended in Coleridge's lines,

> And haply by abstruse research to steal
> From my own nature all the natural man,

could still be an important 'discovery' about the subject; or am I utterly mistaken?

'But how could the existing machinery cope with such a scheme? Who would supervise a purely critical essay? By what standards would it be marked, and accepted or rejected?' I cannot answer this. If the only person who can criticize criticism is a critic, and if there are not enough critics at the universities, a few could be employed. They could do nothing all day long but conduct discussions of fundamental points of critical theory. And in any case I am not saying that this scheme would make life easy for university English faculties; all I am saying is that we might, if we adopted it, stand a chance of getting some useful work done. If a man decided to spend a year writing the best critical essay on, say, Pope, that he was capable of, then instead of telling him that Pope had been 'done', or that half-a-dozen other people were already at work on him, we should simply tell him to go ahead. At the very lowest, and even if his essay were thought not worth a degree, he would at least have been fitting himself for teaching, instead of systematically unfitting himself for it. And is it absolutely settled, once and for all, beyond hope of further discussion, that no one can teach English literature who has not spent some of the vital months of his life attending lectures on the Preservation of Manuscripts, and Gatherings, and Signatures, and how

Elizabethans wrote f's for s's? As it is, we know all about the cancelled pages of the pirated ninth edition of Cudworth's sermons, while vitally important topics, such as — for instance — the whole question of the inter-penetration of literary and moral judgements — have hardly anything written about them.

In these few notes I have perhaps suggested a possible function for the literary critic in the university. As things are at present, it is clear how much use either of them can be to the other. None.

(1955)

THE END